AUSTIN

AUSTIN

---

*A History of the
Capital City*

BY DAVID C. HUMPHREY

TEXAS STATE
HISTORICAL ASSOCIATION

Library of Congress Cataloging-in-Publication Data

Humphrey, David C., 1937–
    Austin : a history of the capital city / by David C. Humphrey.
      p.   cm.   —(Fred Rider Cotten popular history series; no. 10)
    Includes bibliographical references and index.
    ISBN 0-87611-162-2 (alk. paper)
    1. Austin (Tex.)—History. I. University of Texas at Austin. Center for Studies in
    Texas History. II. Title. III. Series.
    F394.A957H857   1997
    976.4'252—dc21
                                                        97-14174
                                                         CIP

Published by the Texas State Historical Association in cooperation with the Center
for Studies in Texas History at the University of Texas at Austin.

Cover: Austin skyline, from the hills west of town. Photograph by Michael A.
Murphy. *Courtesy Texas Department of Transportation.*

CONTENTS

1.
EMBATTLED CAPITAL AND FRONTIER TOWN

ON A JANUARY DAY IN 1840, Alphonse Dubois de Saligny of France and several well-armed escorts set out on horseback from Houston for the frontier village of Austin. For five days they struggled along roads made nearly impassable by the rain. One of Saligny's horses died of exhaustion, and another drowned while crossing the Brazos River. On the third day a sizable band of Indians threatened his party. Finally France's first chargé d'affaires to the fledgling nation of Texas reached the frontier capital that Sam Houston considered "the most unfortunate site upon earth for the Seat of Government."[1]

Founded on the very edge of settlement in 1839 to serve as permanent capital of Texas, Austin fought for thirty-three years to retain that role—against political opponents like Sam Houston, armed enemies on the frontier, and competing Texas towns. Not until 1872 was the issue resolved for good in Austin's favor, vindicating a decision in 1839 that the undaunted Saligny called "as wise and farsighted as it was bold and daring" but that critics thought "ridiculous and absurd."[2]

No one deserves more credit or blame for that decision than Mirabeau B. Lamar, who succeeded Sam Houston as president of the Republic of Texas in December 1838. Envisioning a Texas empire to the west, carved out of lands still in the hands of Mexico and the Comanches, Lamar believed the Colorado River frontier could become the heartland of that empire. Earlier in 1838 he had camped with an escort of Texas Rangers near the point where Shoal Creek flows into the Colorado River. Awakened to word that the prairie was filled with buffalo, Lamar saddled up and shot the biggest buffalo one ranger ever saw at the very spot that became the corner of Congress Avenue and Eighth Street.[3]

The new president had barely taken office when the Texas Congress established a commission to select a permanent site for a capital. Texas's temporary capital, the town of Houston, displeased many legislators, who called it a "wretched mudhole" and claimed that its two principal cultural institutions were the brothel and the gambling house.[4] The new capital was to be named "City of Austin"—in honor of the founder of Anglo-American Texas, Stephen F. Austin—a name adopted by the Texas Senate in lieu of the House's choice, "City of Texas."[5]

In February 1839 the commission headed into the wilderness under instructions from Congress to find a site between the Colorado and Trinity Rivers north of the old San Antonio Road and under instructions from Lamar to visit the Colorado River site where he had camped. There the commissioners found the newly incorporated hamlet of Waterloo with four or so families. No other setting, the commission reported in April, "combined so many and such varied advantages and beauties," from its abundant water and limestone and the salubrity of its climate to the nearby "green romantic Mountains" ("of about three hundred feet elevation"). While located far from the center of population, it was central to the Texas territory and destined to become the hub of great trading routes. The commissioners purchased 7,735 acres comprising Waterloo and adjacent lands along the Colorado.

Lamar promptly dispatched his good friend and political ally, Edwin Waller, to plan the new capital and construct government buildings. By late May Waller and his two surveyors, L. J. Pilie and Charles Schoolfield, were hard at work. Out of the 7,735 acres, they chose a 640-acre site fronting on the Colorado River and placed roughly between two streams flowing southward into the Colorado, Waller Creek on the east and Shoal Creek on the west.

The plan was a grid, fourteen blocks square, a regular pattern of streets typical of new American towns. Bisecting the town was Congress Avenue, conceived as a grand avenue extending northward from the Colorado River through the heart of Austin to "Capitol Square." As directed by Congress, Waller set aside a generous number of blocks for public purposes, among them the sites today of the capitol, Brackenridge Hospital, Wooldridge Park, Republic Square, and Brush Square. The north-south streets were named after Texas rivers and the cross streets, running east-west, after Texas trees. Waller's proposal to designate the cross streets with numbers was rejected at the time but adopted by the city in 1887.[6]

Waller resolved to have the new capital ready by the time Congress convened in November, but his motley crew of 200 workmen toiled under trying conditions—oppressive summer heat, scarce supplies, a scanty diet of dried beef, and the constant threat of Indians. Armed men guarded each party of laborers and pastured work animals. A ten-foot-high stockade was built to protect the animals from nighttime raids. The men were restless and sometimes unruly. When surveyor L. J. Pilie stole $3,500, he was tried by a volunteer jury, convicted, tied to the Liberty Pole, flogged, and "sent adrift."[7]

Nevertheless, a frontier capital emerged out of the wilderness. With time so short, Waller decided on temporary buildings at temporary locations. Log houses for the State Department, War Department, and other government offices soon lined Congress Avenue. The capitol, a rudimentary one-story frame building, was set back from Congress Avenue on a hill at what is now the corner of Colorado and Eighth Streets. Across Congress Avenue on a higher hill (near where St. David's Church now stands), Waller built a two-story frame President's House with a commanding view of the town. In August the first auction of city lots, for prices ranging from $120 to $2,700, was held under a stand of live oak trees in what is now Republic Square. Two months later a wagon train entered town carrying the republic's archives—its land, financial, diplomatic, and other official papers. By mid-October, when Lamar made his grand entry into Austin to much cheering

CITY of AUSTIN THE NEW CAPITAL of TEXAS IN 1840.

Austin in 1840, looking north up Congress Avenue from the Colorado River. Facing Congress Avenue on the hill to the left is Texas's first capitol. On the higher hill to the right is the President's House. Lithograph, 4 x $7^3/_{16}$ inches. *CN 01547d. Courtesy the Center for American History, University of Texas at Austin.*

and a twenty-one-gun salute, government offices had opened for business, and the town had some 700 residents, mostly men, living in log cabins, shanties, and tents.[8]

Congress convened in November, but many legislators arrived in foul moods aggravated by their disagreeable accommodations. Opponents had sniped at Austin since April, complaining that the remote site possessed "none of the advantages of a city" and was reached by roads that were "impassable—not even jackassable."[9] Now Congressmen from eastern Texas, led by Sam Houston, bitterly reproached Lamar for putting the capital deep in Indian country without letting Texans vote on the issue. "Western" men rushed to Austin's defense. For three days they clashed over a bill calling for a nationwide election pitting Austin against a site on the Brazos, but the measure was killed in a close vote.[10]

If infant Austin had many detractors, it also had many admirers. Visitors and settlers raved about the picturesque setting with verdant hills "rising abruptly and boldly up towards the heavens" and the Colorado River "dashing down" past the town. The scenery was "rich—varied—beautiful—sublime," one resident enthused. Already the Austin lifestyle had its devotees. "Dident we live as happily in Austin as we can expect in this world," wrote a young government clerk in 1843, recalling good fellowship, swims in "the cooling waters of the old never-to-be-forgotten Colorado," strolls around town gathering wildflowers, and the "greatest time we ever had"—a daylong "burlesque on Congress."[11]

Yet Austin was also an "Indian haunted community," in the words of one resident.[12] Volunteer guards patrolled the town, alert for raiders usually on the prowl for livestock. When Congress recessed in 1840 and more than half the population of 1,000 or so left town, fear escalated that the Comanches or the Mexicans might attack in force. Lamar decided to fortify the capital to provide a refuge for the citizenry and the archives, but his ambitious plan was denounced as way out of proportion to the threat. So he settled for a five-foot-wide ditch and a stockade around the capitol, which opponents then ridiculed as a plaything for children and named "Lamar's folly."[13]

When Congress reconvened in 1841, the situation had deteriorated. Anxiety over Indian depredations on the frontier—some within hearing and sight of town—was heightened by the growing threat of an invasion from Mexico, which still claimed sovereignty over Texas and resented Lamar's efforts to add territory to Texas at Mexico's expense.[14] But Austin's fate really lay in the hands of Sam Houston, who was inaugurated Lamar's successor as president before a gathering of 1,000 in the capital city in December.

The fatal blow was struck on March 5, 1842, when Mexican troops captured San Antonio. Austin panicked at the news. "Next day nearly all the families left town," recalled one observer. "Teams were pressed for the purpose—Martial Law declared—all the archives were packed and mostly burried."[15] Apprehensive since 1839 that Indians or Mexicans might sack the capital and destroy the national archives—a "calamity" that he believed would overwhelm the young nation and destroy its prospects abroad—President Houston ordered the archives transferred to his namesake city. But in the eyes of Austinites and other western-ers, the move was tantamount to relocating the seat of govern-ment. They responded defiantly, uttering "awful threats and ter-rific declarations."[16] Houston persisted in his demand, even though Mexican troops quickly retreated south of the Rio Grande. He directed all government personnel to report to the city of Houston forthwith or be dismissed.

"We are holding on to the Archives . . . & are determined they shall not be taken from here 'till ordered by a higher power than Sam Houston," the editor of the Austin *City Gazette* assured Mirabeau Lamar.[17] A vigilance committee made good his words. Meanwhile the government resumed operation in Houston, although the General Land Office, unable to function without records, remained in Austin. In September the president picked Washington-on-the-Brazos as interim capital. Not long after, he hatched a plan to seize the Land Office archives.

On the morning of December 30, 1842, twenty-six armed men and three ox-drawn wagons quietly entered Austin and headed for the Land Office, where they were admitted by the land com-missioner, a Houston ally.[18] Col. Thomas Smith presented an order directing the commissioner to dispatch the Land Office papers to Washington-on-the-Brazos. In no time several citizens approached the Land Office and warned Smith that any effort to seize the archives would be resisted. Soon the wagons were loaded with ten boxes of papers. From two blocks away came a cry of "blow the old house to pieces," followed by the thunderous boom of a can-non. Grapeshot perforated the Land Office building. No one was injured, but Colonel Smith and company retreated from town as hastily as their ox-drawn wagons permitted.

All Austin was buzzing as word of the incident spread. Following the meeting with Smith, several townspeople had wheeled a six-pounder cannon into place on Congress Avenue and fired at the Land Office, Angelina Eberly getting credit decades later for putting the torch to the powder. Then they waited for rein-forcements before pursuing Colonel Smith and his party. Some fifty men under the command of Mark B. Lewis finally headed out that afternoon in search of the captured archives, gaining recruits along the way as Travis County citizens rushed to join the chase. Their pace slowed by the nearly two-ton cannon they were hauling, Lewis dispatched an advance party that overtook Smith and his wagons after dark some eighteen miles northeast of Austin. The Austinites yelled through the blackness for Smith to give up the archives. He replied that he was acting under full authority of the president. Both sides decided to wait until morning to settle it. But during the night the balance of power shifted decisively in Austin's favor as the cannon arrived. When dawn broke, Colonel Smith and his men found the six-pounder commanding their position. By New Year's Eve the Land Office papers were back in Austin, where they stayed with the rest of the archives "as a kind of hostage for the return of the government," as one resident phrased it.[19]

Austin relished its victory in what became known as the "Archive War," but it had little else to cheer about. Its population plummeted below 200. A visitor in 1843 found a scene of "desolation"—few of the houses inhabited, the capitol "the abode of bats, lizards, and stray cattle," and the President's House "falling to pieces."[20] Indian raids grew more frequent and more vicious. Residents rushed for the protection of Bullock's Inn on Congress Avenue whenever the alarm drum sounded

Austin's fortunes finally turned in 1845 after seemingly endless political wrangling. A compromise plan to move the executive branch back to Austin was largely superseded by a constitutional convention in Austin in July 1845 that approved the annexation of Texas to the United States and named Austin the state capital until 1850, at which time the voters were to decide its location. The winning town would serve as capital until 1870. Resuming its role as the seat of government in 1845, Austin officially became the state capital on February 19, 1846, the last day for the Republic of Texas.

An "inconsiderable village" with "large expectations," future president Rutherford B. Hayes called Austin during an 1849 visit.[21] Fulfilling those expectations was no easy task, but the stationing of federal troops in Austin and along the Texas frontier after annexation eased the job considerably, eliminating the capital

Congress Avenue in the early 1870s, looking toward the first permanent capitol, completed in 1853. The Old Land Office Building is in the distance to the right. *PICA 02442. Courtesy Austin History Center, Austin Public Library.*

city's troublesome vulnerability to Indian and Mexican enemies. But its future hinged on victory in the 1850 election. Competition was fairly intense, especially from East Texas, where Austin was still considered a distant frontier village (and a "shabby looking" one at that). Public-minded citizens eagerly pledged support, funds, and land for Palestine, Washington-on-the-Brazos, Huntsville, and Tehaucana Hills (east of Waco). Austin counterattacked by emphasizing its central location and the economic advantages to taxpayers of standing pat, and by dispatching a lobbyist to El Paso. Supported mainly by central and western Texans, including 754 of El Paso's 758 voters, Austin won decisively.[22]

Buoyed by its victory, Austin was all the more heartened by the rapid growth that ensued. By mid-decade its population had jumped to 3,000. For the first time the government constructed permanent buildings. The centerpiece was the Greek Revival capitol completed in 1853: a "really imposing building" standing "prominent upon a hill," observed landscape architect Frederick Law Olmsted. But its undistinguished design and dwarf dome later provoked comparisons to "a large sized corn crib with a pumpkin for a dome."[23] Nearby soon stood the Treasury Building, the Land Office (now a museum), and the elegant and graceful Governor's Mansion, still the residence of the Texas chief of state. State-run asylums for deaf, blind, and mentally ill Texans were erected on the fringes of town.

Despite all these signs of permanence, Austin still faced the expiration of the twenty-year term as capital it had won in 1850. The state constitution of 1869 mandated another election, which was set for November 1872. Expecting a pushover, Austin suddenly found itself fighting for its political life when Houston declared its candidacy and offered free land and a half-million-dollar fund for buildings. In response, Austin supporters played a game still a favorite in the capital city—putting down Houston. How unfit a site for the seat of government, it was said of Houston, with its "stagnant, fetid, and green scum-covered bayous." Galveston,

The new capitol in 1892, when Austin was a rustic town of 15,000 people. *CO 1623. Courtesy Austin History Center, Austin Public Library.*

which automatically opposed anything that helped its rival Houston, derided its offer as just another example of the Bayou City's belief that "everything on earth" could be bought. Houston's opponents hammered away at pocketbook issues, raising the specter of higher taxes to pay for moving the capital, and fanned the campaign flames by invoking the race issue, claiming that Houston intended to win by buying black votes. Houstonians fired back, calling the Austin region a "bleak, inhospitable rocky waste" and proclaiming their town the "center of gravity in Texas." Come election day Austin prevailed, winning 64,000 votes to 35,000 for Houston. "The people of Austin all wear bright faces since the capital question has been settled beyond a doubt," asserted the Austin *Statesman*. The new state constitution of 1876 made doubly sure of that, declaring Austin the permanent capital.[24]

Not only was Austin's long struggle finally over, but its triumph was capped by the construction of a new capitol building. The state took the initial steps in 1875, but plans unfolded at a snail's pace. Ground was broken in 1882, the "grand old pile" (as locals called the old capitol) having succumbed to fire the year before.[25] Six years and more than 15,000 carloads of granite later, a magnificent new capitol towered over Austin, symbolizing the town's hard-won identity as the seat of government in Texas.

2.
CONFEDERATE COMMUNITY

ON JULY 18, 1861, 104 MEMBERS of the Tom Green Rifles, their "flag to the breeze," paraded down Congress Avenue and headed east across the Texas prairie for Virginia—the first company of volunteers from Austin and Travis County to join the fight against the Yankees. Not until September 12, almost two months later, did they reach the Confederate capital at Richmond, their journey marked by a 100-mile trek to the nearest railhead at Brenham, a grueling twelve-day march across swampy west Louisiana, and endless days riding and waiting for trains. If the capital city was distant from many settled parts of Texas, it was far more remote from the military struggle that consumed the nation for four years.[26]

Situated on the periphery of the Confederacy, beyond the reach of railroad or telegraph, 1,400 miles from Richmond, and remote even from the war in the West, Austin residents found it impossible to keep abreast of the unfolding conflict. "Its events become history with you before rumors of them reach us," lamented one resident to a friend in Arkansas. The flow of rumors that did reach the capital city—sometimes wildly erroneous reports disguised as reliable news—made an accurate picture of the fighting all the more elusive. In late July 1863, three weeks after the Confederate debacle at Gettysburg, Austin's newspaper was still reassuring its readers that Gen. Robert E. Lee's invasion of the North had produced stupendously successful results, highlighted by the capture of Washington, D.C., and 60,000 Union soldiers. Yet distance from the Civil War and an unremitting flow of muddy and conflicting reports hardly meant that Austinites were disengaged from the conflict. They were absorbed by it, feeling quite rightly that its course and its outcome had profound implications for them.

At stake, first of all, was slavery. Austin was a slave town, just as Texas, with its 200,000 slaves in 1860, was a slave state. Of Austin's 3,500 inhabitants in 1860, about 1,000 were slaves, forming almost 30 percent of the population, a greater percentage than in such Texas cities as Houston and Galveston. More than a third of Austin's white families owned slaves, with slaveowning the rule rather than the exception among the town's prosperous merchants, professional people, and high government officials.[27] Slavery dated from Austin's earliest days. In August 1839 it was reported that "families with their Negroes" were daily seen on their way to the new town. A few months later there were 145 slaves among the 850 or so inhabitants. A slave—indeed, Angelina Eberly's slave—participated in the posse that recaptured the Land Office records on December 31, 1842. Even many of those settlers who did not bring slaves to Austin were accustomed to the institution. Of Travis County's adult white residents in 1850, 70 percent had been born in slave states.[28]

During the 1850s the skill and industry of enslaved blacks played a crucial role in the economy and domestic life of the town. Slaves composed a major part of the work force that constructed the first permanent capitol.[29] They labored as blacksmiths and carpenters, worked for brick masons, wagon makers, store owners, and hotel keepers, and freighted goods. Domestic workers handled household chores from cooking and washing to hauling water and wood and caring for children and vegetable gardens. Some Austin slaves toiled on nearby farms and ranches tending crops and stock and chopping cotton. Six slaves worked Thomas Chapman's 300-acre farm fronting on the Colorado River just a mile from the capitol, where Rainey Street is today. Chapman assured a friend that it was "impossible to work his farm with free labor, it could not be depended on." A significant number of slaves—"nearly half the Negroes in town" according to the Austin *Texas State Gazette* in 1851—hired their own time; that is, they found work on their own, paid a portion of their wages to their owners, and used the rest to sustain themselves and their families, often while living apart from their owners.[30]

On the eve of the Civil War most Austin whites believed that slavery was a legitimate and worthy institution. It was "authorized by time, and custom, and law," maintained secessionist leader and former mayor, John Salmon "Rip" Ford. It tended "to create a perfect equality among white citizens," editorialized John Marshall in his *Texas State Gazette,* since "all menial labor" was "performed by an inferior race." The *Gazette* urged Austinites to defend their social system and their property rights. Both Marshall and Ford feared not just an attack on slavery but a wholesale assault on Southern liberties, but, like many fellow Austinites, they recognized that slavery was at the heart of the conflict.[31]

In January 1861 "Old Rip," riding a white stallion, headed a parade of several hundred secessionists through Austin's principal streets. Yet many Austinites hesitated to follow his lead. Their sentiments were not with the North but with the Union. They deplored the Republican victory in 1860 but opposed efforts to precipitate Texas "into revolution." They organized the "Austin Association for Maintaining Our Rights in the Union" and attracted some of Austin's most prominent citizens to their ranks. "Shall we cut our throat because a tooth aches?" they asked.[32] On February 1, 1861, the Texas Secession Convention voted overwhelmingly for secession, and the Texas electorate supported the decision by more than a three-to-one margin, but persisting doubt about abandoning the Union resulted in a 704 to 450 vote against secession in Travis County. The outbreak of war in April, however, propelled the majority of Austin's still reluctant Unionists into the secessionist camp, although a hard core sat out the war defiantly, incurring the suspicion and periodically the wrath of some townspeople.

Austin quickly "assumed a martial appearance," reported one observer.[33] Within a year more than 600 Austin and Travis County men and boys had volunteered to fight for the Confederacy. As

Robert Emmett Carrington of Austin enlisted in the Travis Rifles at age fifteen and served in the Confederate Army for four years. Ambrotype, $3\frac{1}{4}$ x $2\frac{3}{4}$ inches. *L. D. Carrington Papers. Courtesy the Center for American History, University of Texas at Austin.*

warfare intensified, the town's spirits rose and fell with the reports from the front. News in February 1862 that the Federals had captured Forts Henry and Donelson, puncturing the Confederate defensive line in the West, "made us very low and anxious," Austinite Amelia Barr wrote in her diary. It "stirred us to the bottom here," brooded another citizen. When news (spurious, it turned out) reached town several months later that Union Gen. George B. McClellan's advance on Richmond had been crushed and his army captured, "the town seemed drunk with excitement," Barr recorded. "There was shouting and bell ringing, and the continual cracking of firearms."[34]

With hunger for war news so strong, publisher David Richardson decided in the fall of 1862 to launch a one-page bulletin, the *Texas Almanac Extra*, devoted almost entirely to war reports brought by pony express to Austin from the railhead at Brenham. Three nights a week relay riders carrying the latest Houston and Galveston newspapers in their saddlebags hurried over 100 miles of rough roads, changing horses at stations along the way. When important news was expected from the front, many Austinites lay awake during the early morning hours listening for the sound of the horse's feet. Usually well before dawn the express rider raced into town, and Richardson and his assistants rushed their tri-weekly paper into print while citizens gathered outside the shop.

Austinites followed with particular concern news of the successive Yankee thrusts toward Texas. When reports in late 1862 pointed to a general invasion, an alarmed citizenry gathered at the county courthouse to organize resistance, but the invaders went to Louisiana instead. A year later Federal incursions all along the Texas coast provoked fears that the Yankees would overrun Texas and occupy the capital city. Confederate officials sent a detachment accompanied by 500 slaves to fortify the town. Construction of defense works on the fringes of Austin proceeded through early 1864, but Union troops soon abandoned most of the Texas coast.

If Austin escaped the fighting, daily life was nonetheless directly affected by the conflict. "Very soon I began to really feel the pinch of war," wrote Amelia Barr. It was often hard to find and increasingly difficult to afford the necessities of life, from flour, bacon, and coffee to candles, paper, and cloth. People made coffee from corn, potatoes, and rye, and used mesquite thorns for pins. At one particularly trying point, in August 1863, the *State Gazette* complained that there was "not a sack of flour, a bushel of meal or grain of any kind, nor a pound of bacon to be purchased in

Austin." Even when shops had goods to sell, their rapidly rising prices put them beyond the reach of many. The price of flour shot up ten-fold in two years. Soaring costs for paper, horses, and feed and problems paying with depreciated Confederate currency forced David Richardson to drop his pony express after a year. Families of absent soldiers suffered grievously. By 1865 it was estimated that 500 such families in Travis County were indigent, yet county relief funds were exhausted.[35]

Painful as it was, the war's economic impact at home paled in comparison to its human devastation on the battlefield. The first casualties were heroes. When sixty-five members of the Tom Green Rifles participated in a charge under heavy fire at the Battle of Gaines's Mill in Virginia in 1862, breaching the enemy line and forcing it into a full retreat, the town swelled with pride at their bravery, quietly accepting the cost of twenty-nine Austin and Travis County men wounded and one killed. But the mounting toll of an increasingly desperate struggle grew depressing. Of the more than seventy members of the Travis Rifles who headed gallantly for war in 1861, two-fifths were dead by 1864 and another two-fifths wounded or otherwise disabled. The collapse of the Confederacy made the loss all the more bitter. "Austin was practically in mourning," recalled one resident. "The women could hardly believe their men had died, been wounded, mutilated, to be beaten, at last."[36]

On July 25, 1865, Union soldiers marched into Austin and quietly took possession of the town. They stayed until 1870. Soon it seemed that life was returning to normal. Merchants had goods to sell, and people had money to buy them. But for black Austinites, life did not return to normal—and for that they were thankful. Slavery lasted in the capital city until June 1865. As late as April 1865, two weeks after Appomattox, a slave had been sold at auction on Congress Avenue.[37] Following emancipation, Austin's African American community entered a period of explosive growth as former slaves migrated to town in search of opportunity and the protection of Federal authority. By 1870 three out of eight Austinites were blacks.

The postwar years were a time of great achievement for

The Hezekiah Haskell family in front of its home in the African American community of Clarksville, just west of town, in the 1880s. *Courtesy Haskell Homestead.*

Austin's African Americans. They established a ring of residential communities on Austin's fringes, including Wheatville about a mile northwest of the capitol, Masontown on the east side of town, and Clarksville west of town, where it endures today. They organized churches, found jobs, started businesses, and patronized schools. They actively participated in the political process—voting, attending political meetings and rallies, and serving as aldermen, policemen, jurors, and militiamen—opportunities which they would find far less open to them in the years following the close of Reconstruction. In an event highlighting their concern with education, more than 100 African American children, led by a military band, marched down Congress Avenue in 1868 to take possession of a new school house built entirely by the voluntary contributions of Austin blacks.[38]

In an 1868 article, the Austin *Daily Republican* celebrated the "novelty" of life in Austin following the upheavals of the Civil War. Not only were the shops on Congress Avenue thronged with eager customers "flush with money," but there was a "free intermingling of colors without misunderstanding." Blacks and whites "pass and repass without collision."[39] Obviously the *Republican* grossly underestimated the depth and persistence of racism in Austin that would lead eventually to full-scale segregation. Yet the Civil War had unquestionably wrought dramatic changes for Austin's African Americans. Indeed, the lives of few Austinites had been untouched by the wrenching experience of the war, and for many the memories of that experience remained poignant for years to come.

3.
THE QUEST FOR
"PERMANENT PROSPERITY"

AT PRECISELY 10:45 A.M. ON CHRISTMAS day, 1871, the sound of a train whistle pierced the crisp morning air as the first locomotive ever to enter Austin crossed the city limits. Eager crowds lining the track cheered lustily, exhilarated that the capital city was connected by rail to Houston and Galveston.[40] At long last it seemed that Austin was about to become the commercial center anticipated by its founders.

The commissioners who selected the site for Austin in 1839 envisioned not just a political city but an "emporium": an entrepôt for the rich agricultural lands of the Colorado and Brazos River valleys and a hub of two great trading routes extending across Texas, one running east-west from Santa Fe to Texas's seaports and another north-south from the Red River valley to Matamoros in Mexico. Austin's earliest Anglo inhabitants shared the vision. One of their favorite pastimes, recalled an early resident, was "to get together and discuss the possibilities of Austin's future. The two favored propositions were 'Opening trade with Santa Fe' and 'the navigation of the Colorado.'"[41] The dream of wresting the lucrative Santa Fe trade from Missouri-based traders died quickly. With an eye to winning the political allegiance of Mexican Santa Fe as well as its trade, Mirabeau Lamar organized an expedition in 1841 that assembled near present-day Round Rock and headed west into uncharted Comanche country—Austin newspapers had predicted a fairly easy trek along "450 miles of good road" through "rich and well watered country abounding in game and bees!" Three excruciating months later, its health and spirit broken by thirst and hunger, the expedition was captured by Mexican soldiers in eastern New Mexico and marched to Mexico City. Penned a contemporary: "A chase of silly hopes and fears, Begun in folly, closed in tears."[42]

Far more attention was devoted to turning the Colorado into a busy avenue of commerce linking the capital city to downstream towns and the gulf. In 1840 merchants began freighting goods short distances by flat-bottomed keelboats, but the citizenry's offer of a cash bonus to the builder of a steamboat went unclaimed. Shoals and low water posed problems, but the major obstacle to long-distance shipping was the raft, a thick tangle of driftwood extending over a five-mile stretch just above the river's mouth at Matagorda. The steamer *Kate Ward* did reach Austin in 1846, but only from La Grange, where it had been built. Nevertheless the entire town turned out to celebrate, and the local newspaper gushed that "the fertile valley of the Colorado is, as it were, unlocked, and the treasures of the 'mountain frontier' will be poured into the lap of commerce." Five years passed before the next—and the last—steamboat reached Austin, also from La Grange. Twenty-five cannon provided a "Texas Salute," and an appreciative citizenry awarded the captain and his crew $600 for their efforts. In an ironic last act in this story, an overeager city council drafted an ordinance regulating wharfage.[43]

Dreams of a navigable Colorado were supplanted by the reality of the railroad. By becoming the westernmost railroad terminus in Texas in 1871 and the only railroad town for scores of miles in most directions, Austin was transformed overnight into a trading center for a vast area. Wagons poured into town from as far away as Coleman County, bringing cotton, hides, wool, and pecans, and departing for home loaded with supplies. Arriving trains brought streams of newcomers, more than doubling the population from 4,400 in 1870 to 10,300 by 1875. Land values skyrocketed, construction boomed, and new businesses sprouted all along Congress Avenue and Pecan (Sixth) Street, leading even the pro-growth

Congress Avenue in 1884, looking south toward the Colorado River from atop a building at Eleventh Street. The mule-powered streetcar line along "the Avenue" began operating in 1875. *CN 04255. Courtesy the Center for American History, University of Texas at Austin.*

Austin *Statesman* to complain that the "din and smoke on the Avenue" were turning Austin into "a second edition of Pittsburgh."[44] A host of civic improvements accompanied the dramatic growth, among them gas street lamps, the first elevated bridge across the Colorado, and the first streetcar line. Soon the mule-drawn cars were carrying 20,000 riders a year. Some citizens predicted a new surge of growth when the International and Great Northern Railroad reached Austin from East Texas in 1876. There was even talk in Washington of building an "Austin-Topolovampo Pacific Railroad," and a bill was introduced in the U.S. Congress to survey the route—but to no avail. Designed to connect Chesapeake Bay with Mexico's Gulf of California (and thus the

Atlantic and Pacific Oceans), the railroad was to run from Austin through Fredericksburg to Presidio and then follow the route of the present-day Chihuahua al Pacifico Railroad to Los Mochis.[45]

By 1876 warning voices in Austin pointed out that newer railroad lines were cutting into the town's sphere of commercial influence and diverting its trade to other communities while Austin capitalists sat on their hands. Wagons that once journeyed many miles to the capital city started heading for closer towns, like Luling, San Antonio, and Round Rock, which all gained their own railroad connections to Houston and other major markets.[46] The capital city stopped growing. Its population in 1880 was only a few hundred more than in 1875. Lethargic efforts to reclaim the lost trade produced only the sixty-mile Austin and Northwestern Railroad to Burnet. Austin entered the 1880s a much more substantial community than a decade earlier, but it failed to sustain the growth that the railroad had sparked. Expectations of fulfilling the commercial vision of Austin's founders and of rivaling other Texas cities for economic leadership fell by the wayside.

If Austin's once bright commercial prospects had dimmed by the opening of the 1880s, the citizens of Texas came to the rescue, choosing it to be the home of the University of Texas (UT). The notion of founding a university in Austin dated from 1839. The same legislation that authorized a commission to designate a permanent capital directed that a site be set aside for a university. Edwin Waller selected a block at the west end of "College Avenue" (Twelfth Street). Surveyor William Sandusky, for reasons that are murky, labeled a tract north of the city limits "College Hill"—and his site became UT's Forty Acres.[47]

Texas politicians haggled intermittently over plans for a university until 1876, when the new state constitution mandated the establishment of a "first class" institution "as soon as practicable," with the voters to decide on its location. Prodded by Gov. Oran Roberts, the legislature faced up to the matter in 1881 and scheduled an election for September. Once again Austin found its future hanging on the outcome of a statewide election. Its fortunes this time were in the eminently capable hands of thirty-four-year-old Alexander Penn Wooldridge. Blessed with keen intelligence and prodigious energy, Wooldridge distinguished himself in legal circles soon after moving to Austin in 1872, and just months earlier had led a successful effort to found the city's public school system. Now he took command of Austin's election campaign, heading a committee of prominent citizens that lobbied hard for the university. They flooded Texas with pro-Austin literature, conducted statewide speaking tours, and garnered endorsements from the majority of Texas newspapers. Waco and Tyler emerged as Austin's main rivals, while Houston and Galveston contested for the medical branch, if the voters decided (as they could and did) to locate it separately.[48]

The electorate was apathetic—the turnout rate was a meager 18 percent—but this seemed not to discourage the campaigners nor to soften the pointed rhetoric, much of it directed at Austin. In one of the more hysterical examples, the Tyler *Courier* warned of "drunken legislators, Mexican fandangoes, and Austin mosquitoes" and claimed that the glitter of Austin's limestone buildings was so blindingly bright "that green goggles for the eyes are peddled like peanuts upon the streets!" A spokesman for Lampasas, a minor contender, declared Austin's candidacy "simply another scheme to enable her to live upon public pap." Others feared that a university in the capital city would fall prey to the political whims of the legislature and become the "tinker shop for forging the thunderbolts of partisan warfare."[49] Austin backers stressed that the capital city alone belonged to all Texans and that Texas's revered founders had wanted the university there. On election day voters in East Texas backed Tyler strongly, but Austin prevailed, marking a major turning point in its history. The seat of government was about to become a seat of education.

Austinites were thrilled by the victory but did not find it an instant boost to their economy. The university was strapped for funds from the outset, to the point that several regents questioned whether it made sense to proceed with the undertaking. Governor Roberts asked a special legislative session in 1882 to address the problem, insisting that otherwise the university would "drag along in comparative insignificance for years to come." The legislature balked. The regents approved the design for a capacious

The University of Texas campus and Old Main about 1905. *PICA 07876. Courtesy Austin History Center, Austin Public Library.*

university building but could only afford one wing.[50] Nevertheless the regents moved boldly forward, planning the liberal arts and law departments, hiring a distinguished faculty, and laying the cornerstone for Old Main at a splendid ceremony on College Hill. The University opened in September 1883 and attracted an average of 243 students a year during the 1880s, almost 20 percent of them women. In a trice the regents encountered charges of sexism. The University's initial prospectus announced that men could enter at age sixteen but women not until seventeen. The Austin *Statesman* proclaimed the distinction unconstitutional and an expression of conscious sex discrimination. The board revised its regulations.[51]

Soon UT's four-story Old Main commanded north Austin. Matching it atop a hill on the east side of town was Tillotson Institute's five-story Allen Hall. Founded by the New York–based American Missionary Association to provide educational opportunities for blacks following emancipation, Tillotson Collegiate and

Normal Institute had opened in 1881 at a site that is now the campus of Huston-Tillotson College. Overlooking Austin from a hill south of the Colorado River by 1889 stood another imposing edifice, St. Edward's College. Started about 1881 by the Congregation of the Holy Cross, a Catholic order, the school had been chartered as a college in 1885.

Taken with its new role as a seat of education, Austin began touting itself as the coming "American Oxford of the Southwest" and "Athens of the West."[52] A. P. Wooldridge provided a more sober assessment of the situation in a letter published in the Austin *Statesman* on New Year's Day, 1888. "Our community as a whole, is a poor one," Wooldridge wrote, and "becoming poorer every day." Austin had reached its limits as a seat of government and education, he contended, while its manufacturers were "few and unimportant and our commerce insignificant." "What is to be done to establish permanent prosperity?" Wooldridge asked. His answer was to build a dam across the Colorado to provide water power for manufacturing and (an idea he soon dropped) water for irrigation.[53]

Austin had good reason to heed Wooldridge's counsel. Its economy was faltering and its population edging downward at a time when other Texas cities were booming—Dallas's population exploded 268 percent during the 1880s and Fort Worth's 246 percent. But a hesitant townspeople mulled over the project without acting, snubbing Wooldridge's proposal to form a private dam and power company. So the resourceful proponents of the dam devised a way to construct it with public funds. While Austin was not authorized to finance projects for private industry, it was empowered to supply its citizens with electricity and water, heretofore furnished by a private company whose service and rates many were unhappy about. Suppose the city built its own electric and water system, used a dam for power, and leased excess waterpower to manufacturers. Influential Austinites endorsed the proposal and put forward a solid "dam man," John McDonald, as candidate for mayor in the December 1889 election. The *Statesman* painted rosy pictures of Austin "resounding with the noise of factories" lining the Colorado and claimed that a

The Austin Dam, completed in 1893, and Lake McDonald. The steamer *Ben Hur* is docked at the right. Tom Miller Dam was later constructed at the same site. *PICA 03851. Courtesy Austin History Center, Austin Public Library.*

"boom" for McDonald was "rushing through the city like a Johnstown flood," an inadvertently prophetic metaphor.[54]

The McDonald forces triumphed and promptly moved "damward," unveiling a plan for a sixty-foot-high dam at the present site of Tom Miller Dam that was projected to cost nine times what they had predicted during the campaign and generate 14,636 horsepower—enough to handle the city's water and electric needs and still leave 12,000 horsepower for a dozen or so good-sized factories! Without blinking, a smitten citizenry approved a huge bond issue by a twenty-seven-to-one ratio. "The people seem to have gone wild" about the dam, commented Austin entrepreneur E. C. Bartholomew. They "think it the panacea for all the dull times we have had."[55]

Completed in 1893, the magnificent Austin Dam and Lake

McDonald stretching ribbon-like twenty miles behind it captivated Austinites. The lake became home to sailboats, steam yachts, the three-decked steamer *Ben Hur*, and international rowing regattas. A booming excursion business entertained passengers with moonlight cruises and sightseeing trips. By 1895 dam-generated electricity began powering the city water and light system and the electric streetcar line. Austin was bathed in "perpetual nighttime moonglow" by the city's thirty-one brand-new light towers (more than half of which survive today). Civic pride ran strong at a time when the city also enjoyed the talents of sculptress Elisabet Ney, whose statues of Stephen F. Austin and Sam Houston grace both the Texas and U.S. capitols, and writer William Sydney Porter (O. Henry), whose humorous newspaper, *Rolling Stone*, poked fun at Austin. To town boosters who crowed about Austin's superiority as a resort, Porter retorted that Austin

Sculptress Elisabet Ney in her Hyde Park studio in 1900, working on a bust of William Jennings Bryan. Her studio and home are now the Elisabet Ney Museum. *CN 02910. Courtesy the Center for American History, University of Texas at Austin.*

was "bound to become a summer resort for people who can't get away for a vacation."[56]

While pleased with its achievements, Austin failed miserably to sell itself to others, notwithstanding promotional pamphlets with titles like *Austin, Texas, The Future Great Manufacturing Center of the South*. No one seriously considered locating a large factory in Austin. In fact, given the rapidly increasing reliance on steam power across the United States, entrepreneurs no longer considered power supply a major issue in deciding where to locate factories. In any case, Austin's vaunted waterpower turned out to be a chimera. More than two-fifths of the time between 1897 and 1899 the lake level fell below the crest of the dam, often ten feet or more, resulting in disruptive power shortfalls. Mules were trotted out to pull the electric streetcars and the tower lights went dark. Some weeks the city stopped generating electricity altogether and its "dew plant" halted water service. Studies revealed that the planners of the dam had wildly overestimated the minimum flow of the river and underestimated evaporation from the lake. When the flow of the river was low, as was often the case, the dam produced only one-sixth the power promised.

At 11:20 a.m. on April 6, 1900, the dam collapsed after a torrential rain. An avalanche of water poured through the break, drowned eight people in the powerhouse, and swept down the river washing away homes, barns, and livestock. With it went the last vestige of Austin's nineteenth-century dream of becoming a manufacturing center. Austin entered the twentieth century still searching for "permanent prosperity."

4.
LAST DAYS OF THE FRONTIER TOWN

IN 1878 AUSTIN'S CITY FATHERS, concerned about the large number of people carrying deadly weapons and the "promiscuous firing of guns and pistols" occurring almost nightly, decided it was high time to outlaw the discharge of firearms in the city. And so Austin took another step away from its frontier origins. Yet the capital city retained a frontier flavor into the 1890s. Cowboys were familiar figures, and horses tied to hitching posts lined dusty Congress Avenue (it was not paved until 1905). Along the east side of the Avenue the saloons, cowmen, and gamblers were so thick in the evenings that "ladies" would not think of walking there.[57] Gambling was "alarmingly prevalent" according to an 1892 publication of the Chicago-based Anti-Gambling Association, befitting a town that in the 1870s and 1880s became the headquarters of the Texas "sporting"crowd (as the gambling fraternity was known), outshining even Fort Worth and San Antonio. Indeed, the town that could not attract factories was a magnet to "top-notch night rounders" of all kinds. "Austin was a gay place," recalled one resident, "filled with cowmen, flush of money, rearing to spend it on gambling, booze, and the women of the night."[58]

The capital city was born a lively frontier town. When only months old, it had nine saloons and six gambling operations. In 1849 Rutherford B. Hayes found "gaming and drinking very abounding in all quarters," and visitors during the 1850s were no

Cowboys Tom Bird and John James Haynes at photographer William J. Oliphant's Gallery on East Pecan (Sixth) Street about 1868. Bird, who later became a Texas Ranger, froze to death in a Texas blizzard. Haynes ranched in Blanco County and made thousands of dollars driving cattle to Kansas. Albumen carte de visite. *Courtesy Lawrence T. Jones Collection.*

less struck by the "very remarkable number of drinking and gambling shops." A legislator confided to his wife in 1853 that there was "as much drinking & gambling as any place I ever saw."[59] During the 1860s the first houses of prostitution appeared—and in 1870 a futile city ordinance making them illegal. The opportunities to enjoy "gambling, booze, and the women of the night" multiplied in the 1870s following the coming of the railroad and the boom that ensued.

A favorite nighttime haunt during the late nineteenth century was Guy Town, an area just west of Congress Avenue and south of Pine (Fifth) Street that housed close to 100 prostitutes by 1880. To Guy Town flocked townsmen and visitors alike—from gamblers and ranch hands to politicians and University of Texas students. When the legislature was in session, madams like Blanche Dumont and Georgia Fraser hired extra women to handle the business. Dixie Darnelle named the rooms in her house after nearby towns—the Llano Room, the Marble Falls Room—so that the boys from the Hill Country would feel at home. Guy Town's popularity was made plain in an incident reported in the local newspaper in 1877. Thirty-seven-year-old Fanny Kelley, proprietress of a "high-tone bagnio" in Guy Town, stood before the mayor's court charged with keeping a house of ill fame. The city attorney called to the witness stand Officer Sheehan of the city police force. Please tell the court where Fanny Kelley's house is located, requested the attorney. "Now what are you after asking me such a question as that for?" snapped back Sheehan. "Yerself and every man on that jury know as well as meself where Fanny Kelley's is, and yeve all been thar often."[60]

Guy Town's many saloons included Polo's, the "hardest dump that Austin has ever seen" according to a policeman familiar with the scene. A few blocks to the west was Charlie Cooney's notorious saloon and fandango house. But far better known were drinking establishments like the Iron Front and the Crystal that flourished on Congress Avenue and along Pecan (Sixth) Street. Austin had eighty saloons by the 1880s. The better establishments lured customers with choice liquors, fresh cool beer, Havana cigars, free lunches, billiard tables, and private rooms. "I will never forget the

Georgia Fraser's illustrious bawdy house, located at the corner or West Second and Colorado Streets, about 1900. *Courtesy Austin History Center, Austin Public Library.*

times we used to have in the back room of the old Iron Front," recalled a local patron, "some of the best times men ever had."[61]

On the second floor above the saloons, gambling dens ran "full blast" every night. William Sydney Porter and his hard-drinking cronies spent many an evening enjoying Austin's watering holes and playing faro, chuckaluck, keno, stud poker, and roulette. In 1887 there were reports that no less than twenty poker rooms were busy entertaining the current crop of legislators. The Crystal and the Iron Front attracted some of Texas's most infamous gamblers and gunmen. Austin's very own Ben Thompson, of whom Bat Masterson said that it was doubtful "if in his time there was another man living who equalled him with a pistol in a life-and-death struggle," ran gambling operations at the Iron Front. Gamblers were reputed to have strong political influence in the town, and they undoubtedly had ties to the police. Thompson himself served as city marshal from 1880 to 1882.[62]

As the century neared its close, Austin's frontier character faded. "Bad men are out of date in Austin," quipped William Sydney Porter in 1894. "Our city marshal wears broadcloth clothes, a white tie, and never carries his gun, except at meetings of the city council."[63] The buildings that for decades housed the Iron Front and Crystal Saloons were demolished about 1910 to make way for eight-story office buildings, Austin's first "skyscrapers." Guy Town was closed in 1913. Austin's frontier past soon became just a memory.

A segregated restroom in the Travis County Courthouse. *AS-60-26463-1. Courtesy Austin History Center, Austin Public Library.*

5.
THE DIVIDED
COMMUNITY

IN DECEMBER 1885 THE WHITE citizens of Austin's seventh ward organized an "Anti-Colored Movement" to prevent the reelection of Albert Carrington, the black city council member elected to represent the biracial ward two years earlier. A week later the fourth African American to sit on the city council since the Civil War lost his seat—and became the last black council member for eighty-six years, until 1971. "This is white man's country," proclaimed the Austin *Statesman* in 1927, during an era that saw blacks subjected to pervasive discrimination and an increasingly rigid system of segregation. Whites "will tolerate no idea of social equality," a black audience was warned in 1919 by A. P. Wooldridge, who had just stepped down after ten years as mayor. Similar treatment was extended to Austin's Mexican immigrants as they transformed the town from a biracial to a tri-ethnic community during the 1920s and the 1930s. Not until mid-century did segregation come under serious attack—and then it took years of struggle to undermine it.[64]

At the opening of the twentieth century the segregation of Austin's 5,800 African American residents (26 percent of the population) was fairly widespread. "There is a distinct color line," pronounced the city's Board of Trade in the 1890s. Blacks and whites were assigned to separate public schools, as mandated by state law. The University of Texas admitted whites only, while blacks attended Tillotson College and Samuel Huston College once it opened in 1900. Many a gathering place and public accommodation patronized by whites excluded African Americans. "None but the best white society will be admitted," advertised Scholz Garden.[65]

During the first three decades of the twentieth century the lines of separation hardened as Jim Crow laws and practices proliferated. In 1906 the city council passed an ordinance requiring separate compartments for African Americans and whites on streetcars, provoking a three-month streetcar boycott by an angry black community. The last few seats of each car were turned backwards and designated "For Colored." African Americans occasionally flouted the ordinance—violent conflicts with motormen enforcing it were not unknown—but for the most part separate seating was maintained and later extended to buses.[66]

Residential segregation accelerated during the same years. In 1880 African Americans were widely scattered across the city, living in virtually every neighborhood in addition to several suburban black communities. By 1910 blacks had begun to congregate on the east side of town, and, by 1930, 80 percent lived in a single distinct ethnic cluster in East Austin. Black residents and newcomers alike gravitated to East Austin as it developed its own business, social, and religious life and became a haven from white oppression. But residential segregation was less a matter of choice than of imposition. "Exclusively for White People" declared an advertisement for the residential community of Hyde Park at the turn of the century. By the 1920s deed restrictions had given such sentiments legal standing, and their widespread use prohibited blacks from buying or renting property in many neighborhoods outside East Austin. In 1928, following two years of discussions among Texas city planners about how to impose residential segregation officially, the city council adopted a comprehensive "City Plan" that called for making East Austin a "negro district." Municipal services for African Americans were to be confined to the district "as an incentive to draw the negro population." The city parks board established Rosewood Park "for Colored" in East Austin but kept other city parks closed to blacks. Sewer service was extended to East Austin by 1930 but denied to the westside black enclaves of Clarksville and Wheatville. East Austin's Anderson High School, established in 1907, remained the only high school for African Americans for half a century.[67]

On top of narrowing residential options, African Americans were subjected to inferior public services. Black public schools struggled with rundown buildings, overcrowded classrooms, "starvation salaries" for teachers, hand-me-down books, and a school system that readily admitted it spent far more per pupil to educate whites than blacks. The City Hospital annex, to which African American patients were relegated, was declared "unsuitable for hospital uses" by the city physician in 1920 because of overcrowding, poor ventilation and lighting, falling plaster, and rodent and parasite infestation but remained in service until 1928. Second-rate care for blacks in the newly constructed, segregated wing of City Hospital (renamed Brackenridge Hospital in 1933) lasted into the 1950s.[68]

And then there were the daily indignities that African Americans endured in white-dominated parts of town. Such a seemingly simple matter as finding a drink of water on a hot day was problematic, especially after Constable Charles Hamby conducted a one-man campaign in 1921 to stamp out "drinking fountain racial equality," assaulting more than a dozen African Americans over several weeks who were drinking out of the public fountain on Congress Avenue. "Colored Only" rest rooms were even more scarce than "Colored Only" fountains. When Dr. Connie Yerwood began working in 1937 for the Texas Public Health Service, she had to walk some ten blocks to her East Austin home to use the rest room. The only movie theater outside East Austin that admitted blacks—the Ritz Theatre on Sixth Street—restricted them to the balcony while the better seats downstairs went to whites. An African American woman shopping downtown was welcomed by some white proprietors but not by most of those on Congress Avenue. If given the rare privilege of shopping at an upscale store like Scarbrough's, she would be allowed to try on a hat only if she first covered her hair with paper, and if she wanted to buy a dress she would not be permitted to try it on at

Delashwah's Drug Store at 421 East Sixth Street in the 1920s. Proprietor Thomas Delashwah is on the right. *CN 02962. Courtesy the Center for American History, University of Texas at Austin.*

all, unless, perhaps, she was one of a handful of special servants. A bite to eat at one of Congress Avenue's coffee shops was out of the question.[69]

The African American community was by no means without its own alternatives. A racially mixed commercial district on East Sixth Street dating from the late nineteenth century featured a variety of black proprietors and professional people. In 1924, for instance, the four-block stretch starting at San Jacinto Street included some twenty black-run businesses, ranging from restaurants and barber shops to a millinery, a grocery, and a drug store, in addition to the offices of six physicians and dentists, a lawyer, several mutual aid and fraternal associations, and the enterprises of the Reverend Lee Campbell, pastor of Ebenezer Baptist Church, including his weekly newspaper, *The Herald*. The National Negro Business League had three branches in the Austin area by the 1920s. By mid-century the capital city had more than 150 black-owned small businesses.[70]

African American businessmen and medical professionals joined ministers (Austin had thirty-six black churches by 1940) and educators in forming a black elite, but large numbers of blacks toiled in unskilled and low-paying jobs. Early in the century many worked as field hands on Travis County farms. In fact, seasonal jobs for families picking cotton normally drained black city schools of students in the fall. By 1930 few Austin blacks still worked in the fields, but skilled urban jobs were hard to come by both for African Americans and for women, and women composed half the black workforce. While a quarter of the men worked in construction and retailing, half the workforce and 80 percent of the women were in domestic service.[71]

Although subjected to systematic discrimination by whites, African Americans did not take to the streets in protest. The day-to-day struggle just to earn enough to live on consumed the energies of many, and grievances were sometimes muted by the bonds that developed between white families and black help. Moreover, political action was risky when whites had such an overpowering upper hand. In 1918 blacks organized a local chapter of the National Association for the Advancement of Colored People, but state officials ordered it disbanded the next year. When John Shillady, the NAACP's white executive secretary, came to Austin to assist the chapter, he was severely beaten by several white residents (including a county judge) and ordered out of town. The chapter's chief officer was arrested. The chapter languished. The white man "knows his power and will not hesitate to use it," A. P. Wooldridge told an African American audience following the incident. Two years later white intimidation of African Americans took a different form with the establishment of Capital City Klan No. 81 and a parade by 500 white-robed and hooded Ku Klux Klansmen on Congress Avenue.[72]

Some leaders in the African American community, in particular the Reverend Campbell, its dominant voice until his death in 1927, preached accommodation with whites, advising blacks to "stay in their places." But others pushed a more activist stance. By the late 1920s black leaders had forged a unified political front that began to capitalize on the community's modest political leverage:

although burdened with a poll tax that kept many from voting, African Americans voted in large enough numbers to be a critical factor in close political contests and in votes on major bond issues. Under the leadership of Everett H. Givens, a successful dentist and a soft-spoken but tireless advocate of improvements for East Austin, African Americans began asking for—and getting—concessions from white politicians, from a new junior high school and a "Negro Branch Library" to better sanitation and hospital facilities.[73]

During World War I many Austin blacks headed north for jobs made available when the war dried up European immigration. Austin area employers, particularly Travis County farmers, started tapping a new labor pool: the many thousands of Mexican immigrants fleeing revolutionary turmoil in their homeland in search of work and food in Texas. Mexicans had first migrated to the Austin area before the Civil War, but in small numbers that were reduced to a handful in 1854 when a vigilance committee expelled about twenty families camped near town for instilling "false notions of freedom" in slaves. By 1875 Mexican immigrants had founded a permanent community of some 300 residents, concentrated west of lower Congress Avenue near the mouth of Shoal Creek. In 1900 Mexican Americans still numbered just a few hundred, but by 1930 their population had mushroomed to 5,000—almost 10 percent of Austin's inhabitants.[74]

Austin area employers quickly grew dependent on the city's Mexican American laborers. Displacing blacks on Travis County farms, at least half may have toiled in the fields for at least part of the year in 1930. In town they worked at a great variety of mostly low-paying and often temporary jobs, many businesses employing children at token wages. The same years also saw the beginnings of a thriving Mexican American food industry embracing food stores, bakeries, restaurants, and Crescenciano Segovia's Austin Tortilla Manufacturing Company, which produced several thousand tortillas a day during the 1930s for customers as far away as New York. In 1931 Roy Velasquez started Roy's Taxi, a business that prospered and became a launching pad for his community leadership.[75]

Cabs of Roy's Taxi in front of Moreno Service Station on East Sixth Street in 1936. Roy Velasquez is third from the left. *Courtesy Moreno Family.*

Increasingly an integral part of Austin's economy, Mexican Americans nevertheless did not shake the image that whites had long had of them as outsiders, an image sustained not just by foreign birth and a foreign tongue but also by the frequency with which many moved in and out of town in tune with seasonal work in the fields. Mayor Wooldridge complained that their "coming and going" increased contagious diseases in Austin and requested that only whites and African Americans be employed in a street-repair program so that "local men" would be given preference over Mexicans. As late as 1930 Mexican Americans still were noticeably more transient than whites or blacks. Almost half of those in Austin in 1929 had departed by 1931, a rate of out-migration twice that of whites. Perceived by whites as aliens, Mexican

Americans were also scorned as inferiors. "Mexicans are regarded as on a level with the negroes," editorialized the Austin *American* in 1922.[76]

By 1930 most Mexican Americans lived either in the sixty-year-old "Mexican District" near lower Shoal Creek or in the newer but larger barrio on the east side of town. It was natural enough that Mexican immigrants would seek out neighborhoods populated by Spanish-speaking compatriots and dotted with ethnic stores and churches, but whites purposefully narrowed their options through deed restrictions and limits on access to public services, much as they did to blacks. A tri-ethnic pattern of segregation developed with schools, parks, playgrounds, and public housing assigned to each group. Zaragosa Park in the East Austin barrio was designated the "Community Center for all the Mexicans of Austin." Mexican American children attended "Mexican" public schools (ostensibly schools for "non-English-speaking children") through grade three or Mexican parochial schools, played in the city's two East Austin playgrounds "for Mexicans," perhaps on one of the city's softball teams for Mexican boys, and swam in Zaragosa pool. Palm Playground for whites at the corner of East Avenue (now Interstate 35) and East Third Street, with its inviting ball field, swings, slides, and swimming pool, was located only a stone's throw from the home of many Mexican American youngsters, but, as one youth (A. B. Cantu) later recalled, "the playground leader would come up to us and tell us we had to leave, we couldn't play there, we'd have to go to Zaragosa Park." Characteristically, in 1939 the Austin Housing Authority completed three low-rent apartment complexes—Santa Rita for Mexican Americans, Rosewood for African Americans, and Chalmers Court for whites.[77]

Outside their neighborhoods, Mexican Americans encountered widespread discrimination, though it was by no means as far-reaching or rigid as that faced by African Americans. "Them blacks was in a helluva shape, you know?" recalled Roy Velasquez. "God Amighty, we least could eat in some of the restaurants." Nor were Mexican Americans subjected to Jim Crow laws. Children who stayed the course in their underfunded and

The Austin Cardinals baseball team in 1935 with its sponsor, Nash Moreno (back row, center). A Mexican American team, the Cardinals played in Zaragosa Park and the Central Texas area. *Courtesy Moreno Family.*

overcrowded Mexican elementary schools were not barred from moving on to the white school system. Even so, prejudice took a heavy toll. Due largely to discrimination in employment and education, almost 90 percent of Mexican American workers in the late 1940s were limited to unskilled and semiskilled jobs.[78]

Mexican American leaders counterattacked with an aggressive campaign against segregation during the 1940s. "Our first issue was the Brackenridge Hospital" (which segregated Hispanics as well as blacks), recalled Roy Velasquez, "then the parks and swimming pools—we start[ed] hitting City Hall right and left." Forty years later A. B. Cantu vividly remembered the day in 1946 that the barriers fell at Palm Playground pool. "We went down there early in the morning, and went running in full blast, it was all we could think of. No one was going to say, 'Hey Mexican, go away.'" Through negotiation, protests, and court action, Mexican

American leaders made appreciable headway in opening up city facilities and public accommodations, but, handicapped as they were by poor organization and political apathy in the ranks, their gains in areas like employment, housing, and political representation were meager. Not until the 1970s would the first Mexican American win election to political office in Travis County.[79]

Segregation was already under fire from another direction, however. In 1946 a slightly built, soft-spoken man named Heman Marion Sweatt applied for admission to the University of Texas Law School. Rejected solely because he was an African American, he filed a lawsuit against the university with the full backing of the NAACP and with attorney Thurgood Marshall in charge of his case. In 1950 the U.S. Supreme Court ruled in Sweatt's favor. UT began admitting African Americans to selected graduate programs and then in 1956 dropped all racial restrictions on admission, becoming the first major southern university to admit blacks as undergraduates.

Energized by the Sweatt case, Austin blacks began gnawing away at Jim Crow, no longer content with piecemeal handouts for East Austin. In 1951 Tillotson College professor Bill Kirk called for desegregation of the main public library, insisting to the city council that he could find no legal basis for the city's policy. Council member Emma Long later recalled that "there was discussion about well, we can't let them go in and sit there and read in the Library" with black boys in the same room with white girls, "so they decided they'd let them come in and check books out but not use the library per se." Long objected strenuously and finally carried the day by a three-to-two vote.[80]

Austin blacks kept the pressure on during the 1950s and 1960s, led by activist Arthur DeWitty, who had a vision of equal opportunity for all and kept hammering away at it. They pressed the school board into adopting a desegregation plan soon after the landmark Supreme Court decision in 1954. They successfully fought the requirement that African Americans enter buses through the back door and sit in the rear. They desegregated the rest rooms and water fountains in the Travis County Courthouse and forced the Fire Department to hire its first African Americans.[81]

In 1960 UT students took up the cause, inspired by the civil rights movement that caught fire that year across the South. They protested the university's still-segregated dormitories and its all-white varsity athletic teams. On the Drag (the commercial street alongside the campus) they picketed segregated restaurants and staged "stand-ins" that tied up box-office lines at segregated movie theaters. Downtown they joined Huston-Tillotson students and other demonstrators in sit-ins at whites-only lunch counters. Gradually their targets gave way. In 1963 the owner of the popular Night Hawk restaurant chain, Harry Akin, who had begun serving blacks in 1958, persuaded executives for some of Austin's most prominent restaurants to declare their establishments open to all "without discrimination." Within days the Austin Chamber of Commerce endorsed the integration of all hotels, restaurants, and other public accommodations.[82]

By 1964 the structure of segregation was fracturing without the racial strife experienced by many American cities. But the journey toward integration was nonetheless difficult and divisive. A proposal to establish a Human Relations Commission with power to intervene in cases of discrimination provoked a long, bitter, fruitless struggle in the city council during 1964. In 1968 Austin became the first Texas city to adopt a fair-housing ordinance but abandoned it when voters turned thumbs down in a hotly contested referendum. By the 1970s discrimination in public accommodations had become a thing of the past, but discrimination in employment and housing was still common.[83] Few could doubt, however, that race relations had changed dramatically since Jim Crow days, especially after Wilhelmina Delco became the first black ever to win election to the school board in 1968 and Berl Handcox in 1971 became the first African American elected to the city council since 1883.

During the 1950s and for much of the 1960s Mexican Americans played only a minor role in the assault on segregation and discrimination. But the late 1960s and early 1970s brought a political awakening to the barrio that thrust Hispanic grievances into the political spotlight. The sea change was foreshadowed in 1968 by the founding of La Lucha, an activist political group organized by political "nobodies" like Sixto Ramirez and Ernest Nieto. Fed up with East Austin's unpaved and poorly lighted streets and with harassment by the police, they strove to ignite Hispanics behind community issues and candidates, coming heartbreakingly close to electing Santo "Buddy" Ruiz to the city council in 1969. The next year Lucha lined up behind Richard Moya, a candidate for Travis County Commissioner. "Richard didn't know a damn thing about being a candidate," his campaign manager John Treviño admitted later, "and I didn't know a damn thing about being a campaign manager." But with enthusiastic backing from Hispanic voters in East Austin, Moya became the first Mexican American elected to political office in the history of the county.[84]

"For the first time, people have a little different attitude because they know it can be done," remarked Moya in 1972.[85] Other Mexican American politicians followed his lead. With support from an Austin coalition of Hispanics (who numbered forty thousand by 1970), blacks, students, and liberal Anglos, Gus Garcia won election to the school board in 1972, Gonzalo Barrientos to the Texas House of Representatives in 1974, and John Treviño to the city council in 1975, Treviño becoming the first-ever Mexican American city council member. Joining forces with newly empowered black leaders, they became advocates for minorities, seeking to equalize educational and employment opportunities and fighting for more city services and resources for East Austin.

Almost 140 years earlier Texas's leaders had celebrated the birth of the republic and its capital city in a rousing dinner at Bullock's Inn. "Liberty and Justice have here an abiding place," toasted the participants. But from the outset African Americans and Mexican Americans found justice hard to come by. It was only upon moving to San Diego, wrote a black Austinite in 1918, that for the first time in his life he felt like "a free man with a man's privileges and rights."[86] By the 1970s, however, Austin was beginning to live up to the claim made in 1839.

6.
RESIDENTIAL MECCA AND HIGH-TECH HOT SPOT

"WE DO NOT CLAIM THE CAPITAL of Texas to be a great commercial center," Superintendent of Schools Arthur McCallum readily admitted when welcoming visiting groups to the "Athens of the Southwest" during the 1920s and 1930s. "Here in Austin our faith is not altogether in material things. We believe that intelligence is better than industries." A journalist describing Austin for English readers in 1925 compared the capital of Texas to Washington, D.C. "Both cities have an almost indefinable atmosphere of remoteness from immediate affairs of business." Austin's own newspaper characterized the town thus: "center of culture, seat of government and site of the great state university."[87]

Austin during the first half of the twentieth century was by no means oblivious to commerce and manufacturing. Austin jobbers and wholesalers carried on a fairly brisk business in the region, dealing in hardware, dry goods, groceries, and the produce of Austin's agricultural hinterland, leading the ever-exuberant Chamber of Commerce to boast that Austin was the "largest producing point for spinach in the Southwest!" Small manufacturers turned out products for local consumption, while a few larger firms, like those engaged in food processing and the printing and publishing business, shipped products to fairly distant markets, permitting the Chamber to crow that Austin had the "largest chili canning plant west of the Mississippi."[88] Calls were sounded periodically for "more smokestacks" but with none of the fervor that characterized the 1890s, and the Chamber was not especially aggressive about attracting manufacturers, declining to offer special incentives. "We'd like new industries, of course," commented the Chamber's longtime manager, Walter Long, "but I'm not sure it matters much. We get along pretty well as a residential city." The consulting firm that developed Austin's 1928 city plan, which guided city policy for the next two decades, concluded that industrial development would not determine Austin's future character. Instead, blessed with the state government and UT and the beauty and climate of an "ideal residential city," Austin would continue "essentially a cultural and educational center."[89]

It was no mean feat, however, turning the nineteenth-century frontier town into a twentieth-century residential and cultural mecca, especially after the collapse of the vaunted dam in 1900 left Austin saddled with an oppressive debt, underfunded city services, and a public reluctance to approve new bond issues. "Austin doubtless enjoys the distinction of being the only city in Texas that is parkless," groused the *Statesman* in 1908, only slightly exaggerating Austin's plight. The unpaved streets were so muddy, when not dusty, that "an English sparrow cannot fly over them without danger of having its shadow left in the mud," joked the newspaper. In 1905 the city finally paved several blocks of Congress Avenue (and horses fell when drivers unaccustomed to wet pavement went too fast). By 1910 the city had doubled its paved streets—to two, with 300 miles still to go. A few hundred motorists chugged about town by then but not without keeping a sharp eye out for loose cattle, horses, and mules, hundreds of which were rounded up yearly by the supervisor of the city pound. In west Austin scores of hogs ran rampant as citizens ignored the city ordinance restricting each resident to two hogs, penned up.[90]

Public health in the capital city was in a woeful state. Surveys during the 1910s exposed an exceedingly high death rate from tuberculosis, seriously polluted water, meat markets and grocery stores "among the very dirtiest in the entire State," and other deplorable conditions. With many thousands of residents uncon-

Paving Congress Avenue with bricks in 1905, the first city street to be paved. Inspecting the work is the city council. *CO 0606. Courtesy Austin History Center, Austin Public Library.*

nected to sewers, outhouses and cesspools abounded. Garbage and trash accumulated in alleys and was dumped in Waller and Shoal Creeks and along the banks of the Colorado. Housing conditions were "very bad indeed," asserted one survey, with "people crowded together in small huts, one and two families in a one-room shanty" and the city dotted with "many blocks of shanties" that "ought to be destroyed."[91]

Distressed at Austin's civic ineptitude, the Business League, forerunner of the Chamber of Commerce, called on the city in 1908 to scrap its traditional board of aldermen for commission government, a reform already adopted by several Texas cities and hailed for its efficient administration and impressive results. The citizenry agreed, replacing the fourteen part-time, ward-based aldermen with a mayor and four commissioners who were elected at large and responsible for running the five city departments full-time. At the helm was Austin's "foremost citizen," Alexander Wooldridge.

During his ten years as mayor, Wooldridge bubbled over with farsighted ideas for improving Austin, many of which came to fruition well after he stepped down. He sought to establish a system of parks, starting with the conversion of a dismal dump between West Ninth and Tenth Streets into Wooldridge Park, the city's first landscaped public park. He championed a free public library and a city plan that would promote the "comfort, convenience, industry, beauty and happiness of the people," goals he had the satisfaction to see on the verge of achievement before his death in 1930. He proposed a low-water dam below town that would create a "beautiful and accessible lake all along the city front," an idea finally realized in the 1960s. His accomplishments while mayor were less sweeping but by no means insignificant: more than ten miles of paving, better-lighted streets, new sanitary and storm sewers, some small parks, lower water and electric rates, a new hospital—certainly enough in the eyes of fellow citizens to earn plaudits for taking the city out of "the slow, sleepy and insanitary class."[92]

Political antagonists dogged Wooldridge his entire tenure, calling him a spendthrift and his claims of progress deceptive and extravagant. "There is one thing that he is gifted with," declared rival politician Andrew Zilker, "and that is 'gab.'" When Wooldridge stepped down in 1919, his adversaries took over, and civic progress, which had slowed considerably during World War I, came to a halt. Disgruntled opponents of the new regime, led by the Chamber of Commerce and university groups, coalesced behind a movement to replace commission government with council-manager government, another popular reform of the era that retained a small policy-making council chosen at large but delegated administrative responsibility to a professional manager of the council's choosing. Invective flew as pro– and anti–council-manager forces dueled in the newspapers. In a 1924 referendum the council-manager plan won by a mere twenty votes (it remains Austin's form of government today), but the incumbent commissioners refused for two years to call an election under the new charter, until pro–council-manager demonstrators stormed the council chambers and forced their hand.[93]

Austin's new leadership took over a town far short of the "first-class" status it aspired to. According to Adam Johnson, the first city manager, Austin was "badly in debt," its fire department ill-equipped and understaffed, its water and electric system "badly run down," and its hospital "a disgrace." Wooldridge's efforts notwithstanding, the town had only fifteen miles of paved streets and "no parks of any consequence." A U.S. Department of Health survey uncovered such a "deplorable condition from a health standpoint" that city leaders went to great lengths to make sure the report was not publicized. As if that weren't enough, when the new city council asked the chief health officer to resign, he fired four bullets into City Manager Johnson and nearly took his life.[94]

Convinced that making Austin an appealing place to live was essential to its future prosperity, the council moved quickly to reverse the civic tailspin. Innovations long favored by Wooldridge like city planning and beautification became official policy. The 1928 city plan, the first since 1839, proposed an extensive system of parks, playgrounds, and boulevards and a host of other far-sighted ideas. The citizenry was persuaded to approve a massive $4,250,000 bond issue—three times as big as any to date—that pumped funds into streets, sewers, parks, playgrounds, schools, City Hospital, the fire department, the public library, and an airport. Soon a new U.S. Department of Health survey put Austin ahead of all other Texas cities and fifteenth in the nation among cities of its size. Within a decade the new Recreation Department offered myriad recreational opportunities—Zilker Park, Deep Eddy Pool, thirteen neighborhood parks with well-equipped play-grounds, fourteen other small parks, three athletic fields, and Municipal Golf Course—with not a single "Keep Off the Grass" sign. Recreational programs featured everything from athletic leagues to ethnic celebrations to the annual Zilker Park Kite Flying Contest. But for many Austinites the centerpiece and symbol of the new Austin was Barton Springs, the 1,000-foot-long natural pool whose cold, clear water and stately shade trees made it a

Barton Springs in 1947. *CO 1801. Courtesy Austin History Center, Austin Public Library.*

blissful setting for the relaxed lifestyle. "I go to Barton's every afternoon and have a delightful cooling off," declared Austin writer and folklorist Roy Bedichek. "What a poem that place is!"[95]

Austin launched its public improvements program in 1929, the first year of the Great Depression. About the same time the University of Texas went on a building binge, its coffers swollen by petrodollars from oil discovered during the 1920s on its vast West Texas holdings. The University dedicated nine new buildings on its Austin campus in 1933 alone, its fiftieth anniversary year. The 1930s thus began much more auspiciously for Austin than for most American cities—and continued so. "Depression Decade Leaves Austin Transformed; Unmatched Growth of City Revealed by Comparison of 1929 and 1939," trumpeted the *Statesman* on New Year's Day, 1940. By no means did Austin ride out the economic storm unscathed, however. During the early 1930s its economy deteriorated, wages and salaries fell (University of Texas faculty took a 25 percent pay cut), and relief rolls swelled as unemployment grew acute. But compared to the devastating experiences of many industrial and commercial centers, Austin's twin foundations of government and education, together with sizable infusions of federal funds, sustained the town nicely. Its population, in fact, grew at a faster pace than in any decade during the twentieth century, increasing 66 percent from 53,000 to 87,000.[96]

Austin would hardly have fared so well had it not benefited by the uncommon political skills of Tom Miller, Austin's mayor from 1933 to 1949, and Lyndon Johnson, U.S. congressman from the Austin area from 1937 to 1949. The gregarious yet hard-driving Miller took over Austin's reins when the weight of the Depression was heaviest and made a beeline to Washington for the first of many meetings with officials of the New Deal's Public Works Administration (PWA). By 1936 Austin had received more money in PWA loans and grants than any other Texas city during the same period, funding a new round of municipal improvements. Not to be bested, the University of Texas secured its own PWA funds, using a chunk to construct a twenty-seven-story tower that forever altered Austin's skyline. Not everyone was pleased. Writer and UT professor J. Frank Dobie, wondering why a southwestern university should look like Manhattan, proposed that the tower be laid on its side.[97]

But it was Lyndon Johnson who coaxed the most money out of New Deal officials into the Austin area economy—for public housing projects and a host of other civic improvements but principally for a network of Lower Colorado River Authority (LCRA) dams (eventually six) northwest of Austin. The old Austin Dam, partially rebuilt under Mayor Wooldridge but damaged by flooding in 1915 and left unfinished, was completed in 1940 and renamed Tom Miller Dam. Lake Austin stretched twenty miles behind it. Just upriver huge Mansfield Dam, almost three times as high and capable of impounding 100 times as much water, created Lake Travis. The LCRA dams and the Highland Lakes behind them brought enormous benefits to Austin: cheap hydroelectric power,

Mansfield Dam on the Colorado River in 1940, just before the area behind the dam was flooded to create Lake Travis. *Courtesy Lyndon B. Johnson Library, Austin.*

an end to the flooding that had devastated the city in 1935 and on earlier occasions, broadened recreational opportunities that enhanced Austin's appeal as a place to live, and a plentiful water supply, without which the city's later growth would have been unlikely. Austin's economy gained an added federal boost in 1945 when nearby Bergstrom Air Force Base, constructed in 1942 to support the U.S. effort in World War II, was declared a permanent installation.

By mid-century Austin was a fast-growing but still modest-sized community. What many residents (or at least many Anglo residents) later recalled wistfully of those years was its small-town atmosphere, its congenial neighborhoods of older homes within walking distance of downtown, its leisured pace and affordability, its rustic landscapes and green wooded hills, and its very special identity as a political and university community, symbolized by the capitol dome and the UT Tower that monopolized its skyline. Home to Texas's political merry-go-round, it was at the same time a town that nurtured distinguished writers like the nationally renowned folklorist Dobie and historian Walter Prescott Webb. To Webb, Austin was a "magnet, pulling irresistibly at my attention, interest and affection."[98]

By the late 1960s, however, some Austinites had come to fear that "skyrocketing growth" threatened to overwhelm the town they so admired. They complained of streets clogged with traffic, Victorian homes torn down to make room for parking lots, hills leveled for new subdivisions, and high rises that competed with the "proud silhouette of the capitol." Austin was losing its small-town feel, they lamented. And little wonder. By 1970 the "drowsy

The University of Texas in the 1940s, looking northeast toward Mueller Airport, which was still in the country. Memorial Stadium is at the right. Interstate 35 had not yet been constructed. *PICA 19320. Courtesy Austin History Center, Austin Public Library.*

little university town" had a quarter of a million residents and had tripled in population and land area since 1940, thanks largely to the growth spurts of its two traditional economic pillars—government and education. The University of Texas was home to almost 40,000 students by 1970, twice the number ten years earlier and far more people than inhabited the entire city in Mayor Wooldridge's day. Government and university employees had more than quadrupled since 1940. State workers overflowed the capitol, prompting construction of a state-office-building complex just to its north.[99]

But there was also a new factor on Austin's economic horizon that would soon become the engine driving its economy. And what some saw as a disturbing surge of growth during the 1960s would turn out to be just a prelude to fifteen years of eye-popping expansion. C. B. Smith's short-lived but influential Austin Area Economic Development Foundation, established in 1948, foreshadowed and helped shape what was to come. Echoing the words of A. P. Wooldridge sixty years earlier, Smith called on postwar Austin to awaken from its entrepreneurial slumber and broaden its narrow economic base by developing and attracting industry—not the smokestack industry Wooldridge wanted but industry compatible with Austin's special character, like research and development laboratories and "high level" technology manufacturers. While some longtime residents were aghast, others hailed Smith's vision as a "blueprint of its future." Meanwhile Smith's associate, UT engineering professor J. Neils Thompson, an equally adamant proponent of high technology, took the lead in another auspicious development. In the late 1940s the University of Texas acquired a sprawling wartime magnesium plant north of town and transformed it into the Balcones Research Center, a hotbed of scientific laboratories that became the hub of UT's proliferating research programs. Soon UT was spawning R&D firms through its faculty (Tracor becoming the most notable) and turning out a corps of highly trained scientists and engineers.[100]

During the 1950s the Chamber of Commerce took up the cause, setting its sights first on selling industry to Austin. How else, civic groups were asked, could Austin create enough jobs so its children wouldn't keep moving away. How else could a town dependent on tax-free entities like UT and the state government expand its thin tax base? Once support had coalesced, the Chamber began selling Austin to industry, mainly clean industries in tune with UT's research programs, like manufacturers of electrical and scientific equipment. Industry, in turn, found much to like about Austin: UT, the quality of life, the low cost of living, a nonunion reputation, and a location in the booming Sunbelt and in a state renowned for its favorable business climate.[101]

The turning point came in 1967 when Austin landed IBM, the first major U.S. corporation to build a plant in the capital city. Texas Instruments followed in 1969, and numerous "camp followers"—small satellite firms that subcontract to larger companies—came in their wake. They were joined during the 1970s by Motorola and Advanced Micro Devices, and in the early 1980s by Tandem Computers, Abbott Laboratories, and Lockheed Missiles & Space. Meanwhile, homegrown Tracor and its spinoff Radian prospered. Then, in 1983, Austin snared Microelectronics and Computer Technology Corporation (MCC), a consortium of a dozen computer and semiconductor companies formed to conduct joint research and development in competition with Japan and other countries. With fifty-seven cities in the hunt, the surprise victory brought unprecedented national prominence and confirmed Austin's status as a hot spot for high technology. "Silicon Hills" had arrived.

Not all Austin was happy about the turn of events. As the population raced ahead from 250,000 in 1970 to 430,000 in 1985, growing at a faster rate than Houston, Dallas, or San Antonio, the concerns of the late 1960s escalated into a political movement. Some lamented, and others raged, that Austin was becoming less liveable and, worse yet, more like Houston, the ultimate in urban excess—"Houstonization" people called it. Uncontrolled growth, they charged, was jamming Austin's roads, defacing its natural beauty, and polluting its water, even depriving once-pure Barton Springs of its virginity. "They come here, and then they destroy what they came here for," complained the president of the Save Barton Creek Association. As the boom neared its climax in the mid-1980s amidst an orgy of land dealing, it seemed that a town once committed to living well rather than making money was succumbing to greed. A UT professor conducting a poll asked Austinites when the quality of life had been best. Regardless of how long they had lived there, the majority responded that it had been at its best when they arrived and had declined since. A common attitude was: "O.K., I'm aboard, pull up the gangplank."[102]

During the 1970s and 1980s newcomers and old-timers alike rallied to "Keep Austin Austin." Neighborhood groups, which soared in number from three in 1971 to more than 150 in 1983, fought proliferating apartment complexes and increased noise and traffic that threatened the integrity of their residential areas. Environmental groups like the Zilker Park Posse organized a powerful movement to protect streams, lakes, watersheds, and wooded hills from environmental degradation. Historic preservationists, with the Austin Heritage Society in the lead, labored to save Austin's architectural heritage. Once the reformers gained political influence in the mid-1970s they won significant victories, such as the passage of a series of important environmental protection ordinances, the creation of the Historic Landmark Commission, and the adoption of a citizen-originated master plan for controlled growth. They also found that those who held the reins of government could only do so much about growth—certainly not stop it.[103]

What stopped growth—for a few years—was a recession. The frenzy of land speculation and new construction that followed the MCC decision littered the landscape with new buildings, far outpacing demand. The bubble burst in 1986. Thousands of construction jobs disappeared, the office vacancy rate jumped to number one in the nation, population growth stalled, and housing prices tumbled. Government and education, still mainstays of the economy and bigger employers than any other sector until the mid-1990s, kept depression at bay. Austin's coup in landing a second major computer research consortium, Sematech, brightened the bleak economic outlook by the late 1980s, as did entrepreneurial wizard Michael Dell's phenomenal Dell Computer. By the mid-1990s Austin's economy was sizzling again, and once again high technology fueled the boom. When South Korea's gigantic

Samsung Electronics decided to build a plant in Austin in 1996, Austin hailed its new "stature in the global marketplace."[104] Meanwhile, the capital city's population roared past half a million and, together with its "suburbs," the five-county Central Texas region, topped the million mark.

"The question never has been whether Austin will continue to grow," wrote *American-Statesman* reporter Bill Collier in 1979, "but whether it will continue to be a desirable place to live."[105] Despite explosive growth that rendered its small-town charm largely a thing of the past and diluted its identity as a university and political community, Austin in the 1980s and 1990s retained a special appeal as a place to live.[106] People still found it an open-minded, accepting, humane town with an unusually well-educated and well-read populace and a spirited sense of community. Writers still gravitated to Austin, and the life of the mind flourished in events like the annual Austin International Poetry Festival. It was still a town, many felt, where you didn't need to be rich to live well. A profusion of parks, pools, lakes, hills, hike-and-bike trails, and nature preserves still nourished an active, outdoor life. There was still Barton Springs and Sholz Garden and UT football and Hippie Hollow. And there was music. Austin had blossomed into a nationally recognized music center in the 1970s when it became known as the home of progressive country music, and the likes of Willie Nelson and Jerry Jeff Walker entertained at the Armadillo World Headquarters and Austin's many clubs. By the 1990s rock, blues, country, and jazz groups played nightly at dozens of venues, and the town hosted the annual South by Southwest Festival, a music and multimedia conference showcasing some 500 bands. Without blushing, Austin billed itself as the "Live Music Capital of the World."

But for most Texans, Austin was still best known as a political capital, just as its founders had anticipated. In 1839 they envisioned a capital city of which all Texans could be proud, a capital whose "beauty of scenery" and prominence as a commercial crossroads would stir imaginations and "the fire of patriotism." From the outset Austinites relished the sublime setting that captivated the town's founders, but its emergence as a dynamic economic

Willie Nelson performing at the Armadillo World Headquarters in 1972, soon after moving to Austin from Nashville. Photograph by Burton E. Wilson. *Courtesy Burton E. Wilson.*

hub was long coming. And when it came in the 1970s, it divided the community, some cheering Austin's newfound prosperity, others protesting that its price was the very qualities that had made Austin distinctive and appealing. Former Texas governor Oran Roberts had foreseen the problem in the 1890s while a law professor at UT. Speaking out against A. P. Wooldridge's plan to attract manufacturers with cheap water power, Roberts pointed out that the people of Texas had deliberately chosen Austin "as a beautiful and healthful site" for its capital, university, and other public business. Had Austinites "considered how much a city dedicated to such public purposes would be affected by the push and rush of a money-making, crowded population?" Roberts asked. Since the 1970s Austin has faced—and faced up to—that issue, working hard to reconcile its recent economic leap forward with the quality of life it has long treasured.[107]

NOTES

1. Dubois de Saligny to Dalmatia, Jan. 30, 1840, in Nancy N. Barker (ed.), *The French Legation in Texas* (2 vols.; Austin: Texas State Historical Association, 1971–1973), I, 116–117; Sam Houston to Anna Raguet, Dec. 10, 1839, in Amelia M. Williams and Eugene C. Barker (eds.), *The Writings of Sam Houston, 1813–1863* (8 vols.; Austin: Pemberton Press, 1938–1943), II, 322.

2. Dubois de Saligny to Dalmatia, Mar. 17, 1840, in Barker (ed.), *The French Legation*, I, 130; Maurice G. Fulton (ed.), *Diary & Letters of Josiah Gregg: Southwestern Enterprises, 1840–1847* (Norman: University of Oklahoma Press, 1941), 106. This chapter has benefited by Samuel A. Suhler's informative "Significant Questions Relating to the History of Austin, Texas, to 1900" (Ph.D. diss., University of Texas at Austin, 1966), 167–272, and also draws on David C. Humphrey, *Austin: An Illustrated History* (Northridge, Calif.: Windsor Publications, 1985), 21–26, 32–36, 84–87.

3. Alexander W. Terrell, "The City of Austin from 1839 to 1865," *Texas State Historical Association Quarterly* (cited hereafter as *TSHAQ*), XIV (Oct., 1910), 113–114.

4. Kenneth W. Wheeler, *To Wear a City's Crown: The Beginnings of Urban Growth in Texas, 1836–1865* (Cambridge, Mass.: Harvard University Press, 1968), 26; Kenneth Hafertepe, *Abner Cook: Master Builder on the Texas Frontier* (Austin: Texas State Historical Association, 1992), 23–24.

5. The discussion in this and the next five paragraphs draws extensively on Ernest William Winkler's "The Seat of Government of Texas," *TSHAQ*, X (Jan., 1907), 207–245.

6. Edwin Waller to Mirabeau Lamar, July 11, 1839, in Charles A. Gulick et al. (eds.), *The Papers of Mirabeau Buonaparte Lamar* (6 vols.; Austin: Texas State Library, 1921–1928), III, 41 (cited hereafter as *Papers of Lamar*); Hafertepe, *Abner Cook*, 24–26.

7. P. E. Peareson, "Reminiscences of Judge Edwin Waller," *TSHAQ*, IV (July, 1900), 46–48; J. B. Ransom to Mirabeau Lamar, Aug. 13, 1839, in Gulick et al. (eds.), *Papers of Lamar*, III, 62–63. The discussion here and later concerning Indians draws

on the memoirs of two Austin residents from the early 1840s: William C. Walsh's series of articles in the Austin *Statesman*, February–March 1924, "Austin in the Making," copies of which are in the Vertical File for Austin History (Center for American History, University of Texas at Austin; cited hereafter as CAH); and Julia Lee Sinks's series of newspaper articles published about 1878, "Early Days in Texas," copies of which are in her papers at CAH.

8. William S. Red (ed.), "Extracts from the Diary of W. Y. Allen, 1838–1839," *Southwestern Historical Quarterly* (cited hereafter as *SHQ*), XVII (July, 1913), 60.

9. S. A. Roberts to Mirabeau Lamar, July 9, 1839, in Gulick et al. (eds.), *Papers of Lamar*, III, 38.

10. Dubois de Saligny to Dalmatia, Mar. 17, 1840, in Barker (ed.), *The French Legation*, I, 130–131.

11. Robert Potter to friend, Feb. 11, 1840, AF—A8250 (Austin History Center, Austin Public Library; cited hereafter as AHC); W. H. Abell to friend, Apr. 11, 1843, in Alice W. Hardy, "A History of Travis County, 1832–1865" (M.A. thesis, University of Texas at Austin, 1938), 230–233.

12. Sinks, "Early Days in Texas," 5th article.

13. Dubois de Saligny to Thiers, July 26, 1840, in Barker (ed.), *The French Legation*, I, 158–159.

14. Joseph Eve to Robert Perkins Letcher, Nov. 30, 1841, and Joseph Eve to John White, Dec. 29, 1841, in John Milton Nance (ed.), "A Letter Book of Joseph Eve, U.S. Chargé d'Affaires to Texas," *SHQ*, XLIII (Oct., 1939), 213, 217–228.

15. W. H. Abell to friend, Apr. 11, 1843, in Hardy, "A History of Travis County," 231.

16. Sam Houston to Edward Burleson, Apr. 11, 1842, in Williams and Barker (eds.), *The Writings of Sam Houston*, III, 24–25; W. D. Miller to Sam Houston, Mar. 16, 1842, box 1878/3-2, folder 2-45, W. D. Miller Papers (State Archives Division, Texas State Library, Austin).

17. Samuel Whiting to Mirabeau Lamar, Apr. 12, 1842, in Gulick et al. (eds.), *Papers of Lamar*, IV, 5.

18. Humphrey, *Austin*, 34. The best sources on the event described in this and the next four paragraphs are A. E. Skinner's "Mrs. Eberly and that Cannon: Myth-Making in Texas History," *Texas Libraries*, XLIII (Winter, 1981), 155–163; Mark Lewis's account in the *Texas Times* (Galveston), Feb. 11, 1843; Thomas William Ward's letter to Sam Houston, Jan. 8, 1843, in Williams and Barker (eds.), *The Writings of Sam Houston*, III, 230–231; and the affidavit of two land office clerks, Jan. 25, 1843, that Skinner quotes in its entirety.

19. Sinks, "Early Days in Texas," 7th article.

20. W. Eugene Hollon and Ruth Lapham Butler (eds.), *William Bollaert's Texas* (Norman: University of Oklahoma Press, 1956), 195–198.

21. Charles Richard Williams (ed.), *Diary and Letters of Rutherford Birchard Hayes, Nineteenth President of the United States* (5 vols.; Columbus, Ohio: Ohio State Archeological and Historical Society, 1922–1926), I, 259.

22. Ralph Wooster, "Texans Choose a Capital Site, 1850," *Texana*, IV (Winter, 1966), 351–357.

23. Frederick Law Olmsted, *A Journey through Texas* (New York: Dix, Edwards, 1857), 110; *Texas Siftings*, Nov. 12, 1881, AF—Chron (AHC).

24. Austin *Democratic Statesman*, Aug. 29, Sept. 3, 12, 14, 17, Oct. 1, 15, 26, Nov. 12, 1872; Suhler, "Significant Questions," 11, 257, 260–261, 266–272.

25. *General Directory of the City of Austin, Texas for 1877–78* (Austin: Mooney and Morrison, [1877]), 28.

26. This and the next paragraph are based on David C. Humphrey, "A 'Very Muddy and Conflicting' View: The Civil War as Seen from Austin, Texas," *SHQ*, XCIV (Jan., 1991), 369–371.

27. Paul D. Lack, "Slavery and Vigilantism in Austin, Texas, 1840–1860," *SHQ*, LXXXV (July, 1981), 1n., 8; Alice Gracy and Emma Gentry, *Travis County, Texas: The Five Schedules of the 1860 Federal Census* (Austin: Privately published, 1967), 68–70.

28. W. H. Sandusky to H. J. Jewett, Aug. 1839, in Gulick et al. (eds.), *The Papers of Lamar*, III, 91; Names of individuals who took possession of the Archives, folder #39, Thomas William Ward Papers (CAH). The last sentence is based on an examination of the 1850 federal census population schedules for Travis County.

29. Olmsted, *A Journey through Texas*, 114.

30. Ebenezer Swift to William Chapman, Apr. 27, 1850, Chapman Family Papers (CAH); Randolph B. Campbell, *An Empire for Slavery: The Peculiar Institution in Texas, 1821–1865* (Baton Rouge: Louisiana State University Press, 1989), 129; Paul Lack, "Urban Slavery in the Southwest" (Ph.D. diss., Texas Tech University, 1973), *passim*. For a more extensive discussion of slavery in antebellum Austin, see Humphrey, *Austin*, 46–54.

31. Larry Jay Gage, "The Texas Road to Secession and War: John Marshall and the *Texas State Gazette*, 1860–1861," *SHQ*, LXII (Oct., 1958), 198–203; Stephen B. Oates (ed.), *Rip Ford's Texas* (Austin: University of Texas Press, 1963), 313, 314n.–315n., 317.

32. Roger A. Griffin, "Connecticut Yankee in Texas: A Biography of Elisha Marshall Pease" (Ph.D. diss., University of Texas at Austin, 1973), 164–167; Gage, "Texas Road to Secession," 202 .

33. *Clarksville Standard*, May 18, 1861, AF—Chron (AHC).

34. This and the next two paragraphs are based on Humphrey, "A 'Very Muddy and Conflicting' View," 377–378, 382, 384, 389–394, 407.

35. Amelia E. Barr, *All the Days of My Life: An Autobiography* (New York: D. Appleton and Co., 1913), 243–244; James A. Irby, "Confederate Austin, 1861–1865" (M.A. thesis, University of Texas at Austin, 1953), 85–109, 131; *Tri-Weekly State Gazette* (Austin), Aug. 22, 1863.

36. Humphrey, "A 'Very Muddy and Conflicting' View," 389; Mary Starr Barkley, *History of Travis County and Austin, 1839–1899* (Waco: Texian Press, 1963), 337–338; Philip Graham (ed.), "Texas Memoirs of Amelia E. Barr," *SHQ*, LXIX (Apr., 1966), 488.

37. Campbell, *An Empire for Slavery*, 241.

38. Austin *Daily Republican*, Dec. 1, 1868, AF—Chron (AHC).

39. Ibid., Dec. 21, 1868, AF—Chron (AHC).

40. Austin *Democratic Statesman*, Dec. 28, 1871.

41. Walsh, "Austin in the Making," 13th installment.

42. Barker (ed.), *The French Legation*, I, 140n.; George Wilkins Kendall, *Narrative of the Texan Santa Fe Expedition* (Chicago: R. R. Donnelley and Sons, 1929), xix, 74.

43. Comer Clay, "The Colorado River Raft," *SHQ*, L (Apr., 1949), 410–419; Charles Gober from his brother, June 12, 1840, and William Holt to John Trousdale, Apr. 6, 1851, AF—A8250 (AHC).

44. Austin *Democratic Statesman*, July 22, 1875; Austin *Weekly Democratic Statesman*, Apr. 13, 1876.

45. *The Austin-Topolovampo Pacific Railroad Route* (Washington, D.C.: [Government Printing Office], 1875), 8, 13–14. A copy is at CAH.

46. Austin *Weekly Democratic Statesman*, Apr. 13, 1876; Austin *Daily Statesman*, June 17, 1881, AF—Chron (AHC).

47. The discussion in this and the next two paragraphs draws on Suhler, "Significant Questions," 273–317.

48. Ruth Ann Overbeck, *Alexander Penn Wooldridge* (Austin: Von Boeckmann-Jones Co., 1963), 8–21; Roger A. Griffin, "To Establish a University of the First Class," *SHQ*, LXXXVI (Oct., 1982), 139.

49. Austin *Daily Statesman*, July 14, Aug. 17, 1881, AF—Chron (AHC); Suhler, "Significant Questions," 299.

50. Griffin, "To Establish a University of the First Class," 150–152.

51. Ibid., 150–159.

52. *Morrison & Fourmy's General Directory of the City of Austin, 1887–88* (Galveston: Morrison and Fourmy, 1887), 3; Austin *Daily Capitol*, Apr. 9, 1884.

53. Austin *Daily Statesman*, Jan. 1, 1888. The discussion that follows draws on a great variety of primary and secondary sources, prominent among them the following: Austin *Daily Statesman*, 1888–1900 (especially the lengthy history of the dam in the June 8, 1893, issue); AF—Chron (AHC); *Annual Reports of the Mayor and Other Officers of the City of Austin, Texas* for 1887–1897; E. C. Bartholomew's diary (AHC); Thomas U. Taylor, *The Austin Dam* (Austin: University of Texas, 1900); Humphrey, *Austin*, 127–155; Suhler, "Significant Questions," 329–502; Steven J. Kraus, "Water, Sewers and Streets: The Acquisition of Public Utilities in Austin, Texas, 1875–1930" (M.A. thesis, University of Texas at Austin, 1973), 15–56; and Edward A. Sevcik, "Selling the Austin Dam: A Disastrous Experiment in Encouraging Growth," *SHQ*, XCVI (Oct., 1992), 215–240.

54. Sevcik, "Selling the Austin Dam," 220–221; Suhler, "Significant Questions," 390.

55. Austin *Daily Statesman*, June 8, 1893; E. C. Bartholomew diary, May 5, 1890 (AHC).

56. Walter Henry Tips, "The Good Old Days" (AHC), 138; *Rolling Stone*, June 9, 1894, AF—Chron (AHC).

57. Austin City Council, Minute Book B, Nov. 25, 1878, City Clerk's Office; Austin *Daily Statesman*, Aug. 21, 1887, AF—Chron (AHC).

58. John Philip Quinn, *Fools of Fortune or Gambling and Gamblers* (Chicago: Anti-

Gambling Association, 1892), 505; Herbert Asbury, *Sucker's Progress: An Informal History of Gambling in America from the Colonies to Canfield* (New York: Dodd, Mead & Co., 1938), 336; Trueman O'Quinn, "O. Henry in Austin," *SHQ,* XLIII (Oct., 1939), 147.

59. "Austin in 1840," and John B. Mallard to Susan Mallard, Nov. 25, 1853, both in AF—A8250 (AHC); Williams (ed.), *Diary and Letters of Rutherford Birchard Hayes,* I, 260; Olmsted, *A Journey through Texas,* 111.

60. David C. Humphrey, "Prostitution and Public Policy in Austin, Texas, 1870–1915," *SHQ,* LXXXVI (Apr., 1993), 473, 476–480, 495–496.

61. "When 'Four Roses' Was in Flower Here," Austin *Statesman,* Jan. 10, 1926; *Morrison & Fourmy's General Directory of the City of Austin, 1887–88,* 267–268; Austin *Statesman,* July 5, 1909, AF—Saloons, S0319 (AHC).

62. Austin *Statesman,* Aug. 1, 1882, Jan. 14, 1887; O'Quinn, "O. Henry in Austin," 147; Walter Prescott Webb, H. Bailey Carroll, and Eldon Stephen Branda (eds.), *Handbook of Texas* (3 vols.; Austin: Texas State Historical Association, 1952, 1976), II, 773; Quinn, *Fools of Fortune,* 506–507.

63. *Rolling Stone,* May 5, Aug. 11, 1894.

64. Austin *Daily Statesman,* Dec. 3, 4, 1885; J. J. McDonald, "Race Relations in Austin, Texas, c. 1917–1929" (Ph.D. diss., University of Southampton, 1993), 22–23, 104, 110–111; Austin *Statesman,* Sept. 1, 1919. The discussion that follows has benefited immensely from McDonald's illuminating dissertation, which is capsulized in his thoughtful essay, "Community and Identity in a Multiracial Setting: A Case Study of an Early Twentieth-Century American City," Paul Cooke et al. (eds.), *Locating Identity: Essay on Nation, Community and the Self* (Leicester, England: School of Humanities, De Montfort University, 1996).

65. Austin Board of Trade, *The Industrial Advantages of Austin, Texas* (Austin: Board of Trade, 1894), 25; Joe Edgar Manry, "A History of Theatre in Austin, Texas, 1839–1905" (Ph.D. diss., University of Texas at Austin, 1979), 50, 121–122.

66. Austin *Statesman,* Mar. 13, 16, Apr. 8, 9, June 11, 12, 1906; McDonald, "Race Relations in Austin," 148–149.

67. McDonald, "Race Relations in Austin," 112–115, 118–124, 132–142; Austin Human Relations Commission, *Housing Patterns Study: Segregation and Discrimination in Austin, Texas* (Austin: The Commission, May 1979), 7–9 ; Kraus, "Water, Sewers and Streets," 150–154, 184; James Pinkerton, "Struggle of blacks traced in Austin history," Austin *American-Statesman,* Oct. 7, 1984, A11–A12.

68. McDonald, "Race Relations in Austin," 152, 226–231; Anthony M. Orum, *Power, Money & the People: The Making of Modern Austin* (Austin: Texas Monthly Press, 1987), 189–190.

69. McDonald, "Race Relations in Austin," 160; "Doctoring and earning respect" and "The early days of East Austin," Austin *American-Statesman,* Mar. 2, 1986, D29, D41; Orum, *Power, Money & the People,* 189.

70. *Polk's Morrison & Fourmy Austin City Directory, 1924* (Houston: Morrison and Fourmy Directory Co., 1924), 488–489; McDonald, "Race Relations in Austin," 63; John Mason Brewer, *A Pictorial and Historical Souvenir of Negro Life in Austin, Texas, 1950–51* (Austin: n.p., 1951), n.p.

71. McDonald, "Race Relations in Austin," 54, 58–59, 104; Austin *Statesman*, Sept. 5, 1904, Oct. 4, 1908, Oct. 20, 1909.

72. Orum, *Power, Money & the People*, 183, 185; Austin *Statesman*, Sept. 1, 1919, Sept. 3, 1921; McDonald, "Race Relations in Austin," 172, 183–185.

73. McDonald, "Race Relations in Austin," 198–208; Orum, *Power, Money & the People*, 192–194.

74. McDonald, "Race Relations in Austin," 27–32, 49–50, 67, 274; Lack, "Slavery and Vigilantism," 9–11; Joe A. Costa to Thomas B. Wheeler, Schedule of Inhabitants in the City of Austin, Texas, 1875, II (AHC).

75. McDonald, "Race Relations in Austin," 54–60; Earl M. Connell, "The Mexican Population of Austin, Texas" (M.A. thesis, University of Texas at Austin, 1925), 26–27; "Tortilla Manufacturing Company," AF—2500 (6), (AHC).

76. Kraus, "Water, Sewers and Streets," 141; McDonald, "Race Relations in Austin," 47–48, 103, 107–108, 273.

77. McDonald, "Race Relations in Austin," 115–117, 121–124, 136–141, 153–154, 222–225; Annual Report of City Recreation Department, 1934, 1937 (AHC); "Chicano Waves, 1946" *Third Coast*, V (Aug., 1985), 50.

78. Joseph Parker Witherspoon, *Administrative Implementation of Civil Rights* (Austin: University of Texas Press, 1968), 45–46, 51; Robyn Turner, *Austin Originals: Chats with Colorful Characters* (Amarillo: Paramount Publishing, 1982), 144; McDonald, "Race Relations in Austin," 250–251.

79. Turner, *Austin Originals*, 147; "Chicano Waves," 50; Witherspoon, *Administrative Implementation of Civil Rights*, 51.

80. Orum, *Power, Money & the People*, 196–201; interview with Emma Long by Jo O'Neal, June 10, 1974 (AHC), p. 17

81. Orum, *Power, Money & the People*, 198–202, 253–255; Witherspoon, *Administrative Implementation of Civil Rights*, 52–53; Austin *American*, Mar. 1, 1960.

82. Almetris Marsh Duren, *Overcoming: A History of Black Integration at the University of Texas at Austin* (Austin: University of Texas Press, 1979), 7–11; *Texas Observer*, May 6, Dec. 9, 1960, Feb. 18, 1961; Austin *Statesman*, Feb. 16, 1961; Austin *American*, June 8, 13, 1963.

83. Austin Human Relations Commission, *Fourth Annual Report* (Austin: City of Austin, 1973), 12–13, 15–17.

84. Author's interview with Ernest Nieto, May 14, 1985; Alex Avila, "The struggle of La Lucha; the birth of the 'brown political machine' in Austin," *National Hispanic Journal*, III (Spring/Summer, 1984), 8–9; *Daily Texan*, June 18, 1975, Vertical Files-Trevino (CAH).

85. Austin *Citizen*, Feb. 3, 1972, AF—Biography (AHC).

86. McDonald, "Race Relations in Austin," 29.

87. Address to Congress of Mothers, Nov. 5, 1919, and Address to Colored Teachers' State Association of Texas, Nov. 30, 1933, McCallum Family Papers (CAH); London *Times, Texas Supplement*, Mar. 31, 1925, AF—A8255 (1900–1935), (AHC); Austin *American*, Jan. 1, 1926.

88. Austin Chamber of Commerce, *Austin* (Austin: Chamber of Commerce, [1924 ?]),

n.p.; Austin *Statesman*, Jan. 12, 1909, Apr. 30, 1916, AF—Chron (AHC); Howard Blomquist, "Economic Forces in the Growth of Austin, Texas, Since 1920" (M.A. thesis, University of Texas at Austin, 1951), 118; "Austin," *Monthly Business Review, Federal Reserve Bank of Dallas*, XXXVI (Dec. 1, 1951), n.p.

89. Harold A. Stone et al., *City Manager Government in Austin* (Chicago: Public Administration Service, 1939), 7; Koch & Fowler, Consulting Engineers, "A City Plan for Austin, Texas," (Austin Department of Planning reprint, 1957), (AHC), 3.

90. Austin *Statesman*, Feb. 23, 1903, Jan. 3, May 18, 1905, Nov. 20, 1908, June 9, 1909, Jan. 5, 1913, AF—Chron (AHC); Records of Austin Pound, 1910 (AHC).

91. C. E. Terry and F. Schneider, *Social Survey of the City of Austin, Texas* ([New York?]: Seventh Baby Campaign, 1917), 6–7, 19, 27–28; William B. Hamilton, "A Social Survey of Austin," *Bulletin of the University of Texas*, No. 273 (Mar. 15, 1913), 48–60; Austin *Statesman*, Oct. 1, 1913, AF—Chron (AHC).

92. Austin *Statesman*, June 16, 1909, Jan. 7, May 23, Nov. 20, 1912, AF—Chron (AHC); Austin *Statesman*, June 14, 15, 1913, Dec. 31, 1915, Nov. 21, 1926, June 30, 1948; Austin *American*, Mar. 17, 21, 1915, Mar. 24, 1932; A. P. Wooldridge, "Then and Now," A. P. Wooldridge Papers (CAH).

93. Austin *American*, Mar. 17, 1915; Austin *American-Statesman*, Oct. 12, 1930, July 26, 1970, Part VI, p. 7; Stone et al., *City Manager Government*, 3–6, 13–23.

94. Adam Johnson, "A Brief History of Austin's City Government Since the Inauguration of the Council-Manager Form of Government," (typescript; CAH), 1–3; Austin *American*, Mar. 15, 1927.

95. Johnson, "A Brief History of Austin's City Government," 3–4, 8; *Special Report of the City Manager of the City of Austin* (Austin: City of Austin, 1937), 17–35; Humphrey, *Austin*, 183–185; Joe B. Frantz, *The Forty-Acres Follies* (Austin: Texas Monthly Press, 1983), 165.

96. Judith Jenkins Turman, "Austin and the New Deal," in *Texas Cities and the Great Depression*, ed. Robert C. Cotner (Austin: Texas Memorial Museum, 1973), 189–207.

97. Ibid., 202–206; Frantz, *Forty-Acres Follies*, 124.

98. Walter Prescott Webb, "Austin: 'The City of the State,'" AF—8255 (1950s), and the articles in the AF—A8265 (1960s), (AHC).

99. AF—A8265 (1960s), (AHC); City of Austin Department of Planning, *Basic Data: Austin & Travis County* (Austin: City of Austin, 1972), 20, 36.

100. Orum, *Power, Money & the People*, 230–235; "Annual Report," *Austin and Industry*, III (May, 1950), 4; "Austin: Coming Fast as R&D Center," *Industrial Development* (Aug., 1962), 45–54.

101. Dena Marks, "Mr. Gray gives us the big business," *Third Coast*, III (Nov., 1983), 44; Orum, *Power, Money & the People*, 239–241.

102. Toni Mack, "Trading Off," *Forbes*, CXXXII (Sept. 26, 1983), 139; John Taliaferro, "Fallen Idyll," *Texas Monthly*, XV (May, 1988), 114; Molly Ivins, "The university universe," *New York Times Magazine* (Nov. 10, 1974), 52.

103. Jim Shahin, "The Dramatic Rise of the Austin Neighborhood Movement," *Third Coast*, III (Nov., 1983), 98; Humphrey, *Austin*, 233–238; Orum, *Power, Money & the People*, 305.

104. Austin *American-Statesman*, Jan. 17, 1996.

105. Ibid., Apr. 8, 1996.

106. See, for example, Ranch WcWhorter, "Why I Think Austin Is a Better Town Than Houston, Dallas, Paris, London, or Rome," *Southwest Airlines Magazine* (Sept., 1983), 16–22.

107. Winkler, "Seat of Government of Texas," 219–220, 235; Austin *Statesman*, Dec. 1, 1889; Humphrey, *Austin*, 213–214.

INDEX

(Pages with illustrations are indicated in boldface)

Historian David C. Humphrey, author of *Austin: An Illustrated History*, has won awards for his writings on Austin and Texas from the Texas State Historical Association and the East Texas Historical Association. A graduate of Princeton, Harvard, and Northwestern Universities, he lived in Austin for sixteen years while serving as senior archivist at the LBJ Presidential Library. Currently a historian with the U.S. Department of State in Washington, he also taught American History at Carnegie-Mellon University for eleven years. In addition to books on Austin and early American higher education, he has published more than a dozen articles in historical journals, including "A 'Very Muddy and Conflicting' View: The Civil War as Seen from Austin, Texas" and "Prostitution and Public Policy in Austin, Texas, 1870–1915," both of which appeared in the *Southwestern Historical Quarterly*.